CAPONE MAY GO FREE

Book I

A SOCIETY OF POWER

Donald W. Parrillo

CAPONE MAY GO FREE
Book I
A SOCIETY OF POWER

ISBN 978-098256380-9

Copyright © 2009 by Donald W. Parrillo

Published by Capone May Go Free Publishing
Chicago, Illinois

First Edition

Library of Congress Control Number: 2009938000

Printed in the United States of America.

in honor
of my father,
William Parrillo
1903-1952

- Alderman Donald W. Parrillo

"Ah, democracy, I love it!"

"It doesn't matter who votes.
It only matters who counts the votes."

"Let me tell you a story..."

"Everybody had a nickname."

"There's a little thing called
Taylor Street Justice"

"Who in the hell would want to be
Mayor of the City of Chicago
when you can be
Alderman of the First Ward?"

- Alderman Donald W. Parrillo

"The only thing that separates
winners from losers is one word,
timing."

"We're born in sin,
we enter a world of corruption"

"Ivory Soap advertised 99 44/100% pure"
politicians advertised 100% pure."

"Justice should be spelled with a $,
Ju$tice."

"In my opinion, there are only two,
three-letter words that rule the country
and the world; s-e-x and o-i-l."

"I will not write about anybody still living, because I want to go on living."

- Alderman
Donald W. Parrillo

ACKNOWLEDGMENTS

To Morgan, my granddaughter, the inspiration and love of my life.

To my daughter Kim and my son Tim, I am nothing without you.

To my ex-wives, I still love you and always will.

To the First Ward of the City of Chicago, the most powerful ward in the United States.

To democracy, ah, I love it!

I interviewed nobody and researched nothing.
These stories are all my own
true life experiences.
- D.P.

Prologue:

Every word you are about to read is true.

This is truly a true story based on my own experiences, from growing up in Chicago's "Little Italy" where I saw "Taylor Street Justice" administered with an iron hand, to that truly frightening moment when I was approached at my father's grave by the leader of the Chicago Outfit, Sam "the Cigar" Giancana and "asked" to run for Alderman of Chicago's legendary First Ward. That, of course, is the ward that put John F. Kennedy in the White House.

As you will soon read, I was elected, and I was thus in a position to observe the relationship between organized crime, politics and so-called legitimate business. They all came together in the First Ward, and nobody was in a better position to watch the strings get pulled than me, the Alderman.

Friends and law enforcement officials have begged me for years to write a true accounting of what I witnessed. They said I had a special responsibility to tell how the Chicago Outfit controlled everything from presidential elections to Hollywood. They said I was the only who could write such a book, and so I have.

And I promise you that the book you have before you is historic, informative, entertaining, and educational. Yes, educational, because I do hope this book will be read by students of that time in the nation's history when powerful people in Chicago pulled all the strings. I also hope that those with an interest in true crime will read my book as well as anyone who just wants to stay up way past bedtime "reading just one more chapter."

Each chapter of my book is a book in itself, and I intend to expand upon many of the themes of this book into future books.

I have just begun to write!

Donnie W. Parrillo as a young teenager in the old neighborhood, corner of Polk and Oakley.

Friends to Honor Parillo

William (Bill) Parillo, popular Republican committeeman of the 25th ward and member of the Illinois Commerce Commission, will be honored at a dinner next Saturday at the Chicago Towers club. The event, which is a testimonial to Mr. Parillo's personal popularity, will be attended by city and state notables including many of his friends on the West Side. Among those who will be present are Gov. Dwight H. Green, Senator Wayland Brooks, and Wm. John Granata, 27th ward G.O.P. committeeman and member of the Illinois Industrial commission. Harry Gardiner, former president of the Chicago Bar Association, will be toastmaster.

The Parrillo Court Room

A Memorial to
William Parrillo (1903-1952)
Distinguished Attorney
from his son, Robert (Law 1966)

The Parrillo Court Room - at Northwestern University School of Law
A Memorial to Donnie's Father, William Parrillo (1903-1952)

*The night of the great Chicago Snow Storm - campaigning with
Mayor Richard J. Daley at Saint Pius Church, January 26, 1967.*

The political makeup of the First Ward.

Donnie and his former wife Nancy on his 45th birthday.

Donnie's former wife Christina, a swim suit model.

During the 1964 campaign; making a speech in the Projects.

Campaigning in 1964 in the Projects.

Campaigning in 1964 in the Projects.

*The Alderman was also known for his many athletic talents,
including tennis, handball, racquetball and others. He is pictured
above with one of his many trophies.*

Alderman Donald W. Parrillo - City Council Meeting

Table of Contents

Chapter One
PARILLO & ROACH
(THE ADVENTURE BEGINS)
page 1

Chapter Two
THE OLD NEIGHBORHOOD
(A WORLD OF OUR OWN)
page 21

Chapter Three
AL CAPONE ARRIVES
(MAKING OF A KING)
page 47

Chapter Four
THE OUTFIT
(BIRTH OF A MONSTER)
page 77

Chapter Five
SAM GIANCANA
(A NEW BOSS, "THE CIGAR")
page 89

Chapter Six
THE CIGAR WANTS TO SEE YOU
(A TOUGH OFFER TO REFUSE)
page 105

Chapter Seven
THE FIRST WARD
(A WORLD OF ITS OWN)
page 115

Chapter Eight
FROM VICTORY IN WEST VIRGINIA TO DEATH IN DALLAS
(A NEW POLITICAL BARRIER IS BROKEN)
page 125

Chapter Nine
"NO" THEN "YES"
(A CALL FROM BUDDY)
page 135

Chapter Ten
THE CAMPAIGN
("AH, DEMOCRACY! I LOVE IT!")
page 141

Chapter Eleven
POWERFUL UNION
(UNION: POWER TO THE PEOPLE)
page 157

Chapter Twelve
CLAN KENNEDY
(FROM "JOE THE BOOTLEGGER"
TO
"JOE THE AMBASSADOR")
page 167

Chapter Thirteen
THE FBI
(HOOVER AT THE HELM)
page 187

Chapter Fourteen
CAL-NEVA LODGE
(A FUN WEEKEND)
page 203

Chapter Fifteen
THE CIGAR IS EXTINGUISHED
(TAYLOR STREET JUSTICE)
page 215

Chapter Sixteen
POLITICS
(FUTURE SHOCK/FUTURE SCHLOCK)
page 227

CHAPTER ONE

PARRILLO & ROACH
(The Adventure Begins)

William Parrillo would have been Attorney General of the United States had the 1948 Presidential election gone the way the CHICAGO TRIBUNE claimed it went on that infamous first page of theirs.

In 1948, you see, my father and Governor Green went to New York to see Governor Thomas E. Dewey and Dewey's campaign manager, Herbert Brownell, about the forthcoming presidential election. Having been defeated in 1944 by the incumbent wartime president, Franklin D. Roosevelt, Dewey thought he had a good chance in 1948 against Harry S. Truman. But first he had to win the Republican nomination from the conservative Senator from Ohio, Robert A. Taft.

A Northeastern liberal, Dewey wanted to balance his ticket by picking a governor from a conservative Midwestern state to run for Vice President. Dwight H. Green was the perfect choice for Dewey's running mate because Illinois was a conservative state at that time.

So my father and Governor Green agreed with Dewey and Brownell that Green would run for the basically powerless post of Vice President so long as Dewey appointed my father, William Parrillo, Attorney General after he was elected.

My father and Governor Green then rode back to Chicago on the train, and they were met at the station by Illinois State Police Chief Leo Carr who told them to report immediately to CHICAGO TRIBUNE publisher Robert R. McCormick.

A veteran of World War I, Colonel McCormick regarded himself as the keeper of the conservative cause in Illinois, so they went right to his office in the Tribune Tower at 435 N. Michigan Avenue and were met with a tirade. McCormick ranted and raved that he would ruin Green and anyone else who dared to support Dewey over Taft.

Green caved in to Colonel McCormick and, instead of sharing the ticket with Tom Dewey, he agreed to run for a third term as Governor of Illinois. McCormick assured Governor Green and my father that the Republicans would take all offices in 1948. It was their year. The nation was tired of the liberal Democrats and their big spending.

So naturally McCormick wanted Taft on the Republican ticket for President in 1948, but he backed Dewey when he got the nomination, and he

*The victorious Harry S. Truman gladly posed with the Chicago
Tribune's incorrect front page for photographers.*

was so sure of a Republican landslide in November
that he had the TRIBUNE print that famous
headline: DEWEY DEFEATS TRUMAN! The
victorious Harry S. Truman gladly posed with the
CHICAGO TRIBUNE's incorrect front page for
the photographers.

So even if Dwight Green had been on the ticket
with Dewey in 1948, my father still would not have
become Attorney General, because Truman proved
more popular than Robert R. McCormick had
thought. But the nation was ready for a change of
parties in 1952 when voters elected Republican war
hero, Dwight D. Eisenhower, President of the
United States.

And whom should Eisenhower appoint to be
Attorney General but Dewey's campaign manager,
Herbert Brownell. My father would have been a
far better Attorney General, but he was much,
much more than all of that.

William Parrillo was my mentor and hero and the love of my life, and he left us all too soon and too suddenly on January 26, 1952 when he died in my arms of a heart attack. He was only 48, and I was 21, and I can barely make it through the anniversary of his death every year. You don't want to be with me that day, because my father was everything to me, and I miss him still.

And I would be remiss if I did not dedicate this book to him and all that he stood for and accomplished as the son of parents who immigrated from Italy.

That same son of immigrants was seen on the front pages of newspapers when a technicality made it possible for his famous client, Al Capone, to be released early from the federal penitentiary after serving five years of an 11-year sentence for income tax evasion.

My father was quoted as saying he and his partner, Joseph Roach, "would go to work on the new angle" in the case, and that might be all you remember of my father.

But let me tell you who he was and what he accomplished, because he was my rock and my refuge, and his story is the fitting foundation for this book.

My father, you see, graduated from Kent College of Law in Chicago at the young age of 23, which was quite an accomplishment for an Italian kid from Taylor Street. Dad went on to become the youngest Assistant United States District Attorney in the history of the Northeastern District

TECHNICALITY MAY FREE AL CAPONE FROM PRISON

By M. M. MARBERRY

One little, three-letter word—"the"—may result in the release of Al Capone from the island prison of Alcatraz, where he is serving the fifth year of an 11-year sentence, it appeared today.

AS AL LEFT ATLANTA

Al Capone was all smiles as he left Atlanta for first time in six months, en route to U. S. court here. Now, he's a prisoner at Alcatraz island off coast of California.

William Parrillo, Lyman W. Sherwood and Joseph Roach, attorneys for the gangster convicted of income tax evasion, said they would "go to work on the new angle" immediately.

William Parrillo

Shown above is the Chicago Times headline and article highlighting the role of Alderman Donald W. Parrillo's father, William Parrillo in representing Al Capone. The discovery of a legal technicality connected to the use of the word "the" had created the potential for Attorney Parrillo to get Capone released. At the time Capone was serving his fifth year of an eleven year sentence for tax evasion at the island prison of Alcatraz.

To view the entire article please go to our website:
www.caponemaygofree.com.

of Illinois. That was my father, and it was my father, the political powerhouse, who made Dwight H. Green Governor of Illinois.

Allow me to explain:

Dad's partner, Joseph Roach, could have passed for President Franklin D. Roosevelt's identical twin brother. And he played the part to the hilt.

He was, after all, the son of wealthy parents from Terre Haute, Indiana, and he had developed the requisite love of gambling, strong drink, and chasing women. But unlike President Roosevelt, he was a riverboat gambler, and he killed a man.

The story goes that one night he won big and told his bodyguards to leave him with his girlfriend of the moment.

Wrong plan, because that was the night somebody in the know chose to rob him. Although the robber wore a mask, Roach recognized him by the ring, he himself had given him.

Yes, the robber was one of Roach's own bodyguards, and Roach killed him in retaliation, for which he was "awarded" a life sentence in the Indiana State Penitentiary in Michigan City, Indiana.

But Roach's father was a good friend of Indiana Governor Thomas R. Marshall, who later became President Woodrow Wilson's Vice President.

They prevailed upon President Wilson to pardon Joe Roach, who had been using his time behind bars to study law. And so upon his release from prison, Joe Roach was prepared to ace the bar exam and move to Chicago where he turned his recent experiences to defending those charged with federal crimes.

And who should he oppose in those federal courtrooms but my father, William Parrillo, who was prosecuting those same defendants.

My father was immediately impressed by the man with the presidential pardon who had become a successful trial lawyer.

Dad was even more impressed when President Wilson asked Joe Roach to prosecute the Ku Klux Klan in his native Terre Haute.

You don't say no to the President who pardoned you from a life sentence and wrote you a personal check for $1,500, so Joe Roach took his wife of the time back to Terre Haute and aimed his formidable legal guns at the Ku Klux Klan, who were at the peak of their power in Indiana at that time. And you have to realize that those nightriders didn't just go after African-Americans, they attacked Jews and Catholics and recent immigrants as well.

The Klan "thanked" Joe Roach for his troubles by bombing his house and killing his oldest son.

The Klan was tough, but Joe Roach was tougher, and he returned to Chicago to enlist the aid of a formidable ally he had met while he was in the Indiana State Penitentiary: one "Terrible Tommy" Touhy, head of the Touhy Mob that ruled the gambling dens and roadhouses in the northwest suburbs of Chicago.

After his release from prison, Joe Roach became a lawyer, and he used his legal skills to get Terrible

Tommy out of prison, and you can look forward to reading all about Terrible Tommy's exploits later in this book.

So a grateful Terrible Tommy Touhy gladly went back to Terre Haute with Joe Roach and began the counter offensive against the Klan by kidnapping the Terre Haute Chief of Police and beating a confession out of him that implicated 124 closet Klan members.

Joe Roach had each and every one of them indicted and convicted, thus ending the Klan's reign of terror in Terre Haute.

Joe Roach returned to his practice as a defense attorney in Chicago, and that's when he and my father began to admire one another's legal brilliance.

But while Joe Roach and my father were sparring in the federal courtrooms of Chicago, Franklin D. Roosevelt was coming to power and removing all Republicans like my father from the District Attorney Offices.

Seeing what was coming, my father invited Joe Roach to work with him, instead of against him, by forming what was to become the biggest and most successful criminal defense firm in the United States: Parrillo & Roach.

They made the perfect pair of lawyers for Chicago, because my father represented the Italian gangsters, and Joe Roach looked after the Irish mobsters.

Unfortunately, the Italian and Irish gangsters hated each other, and there were many times when

Frank Nitti would be walking out of my father's office while some Irish hoodlum was walking into Joe Roach's office.

It was a wonder they never had a shoot-out in their offices, but it is also a testament to the wisdom and professionalism of those two lawyers, my father William Parrillo and his partner Joe Roach. And, to show how open-minded he was, my father took as his first case a blue-eyed, blonde-haired Irish character named Nolan.

He stood all of 6'5" and appeared on the scene just when my father and Joe Roach were wondering if they had made one big mistake. You see when my father left the District Attorney's office, he and my mother, who worked for the telephone company, had a total life savings of $1,700. And my father had contracted a carpenter to design and remodel his law office so that potential clients would know at once that he was one class act, and that was going to set him back about $8,000.

So my father was watching the workmen finish up and worrying about how to pay them when this big Irishman named Nolan appears out of nowhere and says: "Where can I find Billy Parrillo?"

"I'm Billy Parrillo," my father says.

And Nolan says: "Are you the kid?"

My father nods, and Nolan proceeds to tell him that he just got indicted for the Volstead Act.

And, so you know, even though Prohibition was repealed in 1933, cases against those charged with violating that infamous act criminalizing the manufacture, distribution, and sale of intoxicating beverages went on as late as 1939 and 1940.

Go figure.

Anyway, Nolan says to my astonished father: "I want you to represent me as my defense attorney in this indictment."

And so my father takes a good second look at this Mick smoking a cigar that was worth more than what most people at the time spent on food for a week. Nolan was wearing a grand suit because it cost a grand, and his rock, or diamond ring, was so big that he needed two hands to hold it up.

So my father reckons this big Irishman must have made a fortune during Prohibition, and so he says: "Yes, I'll represent you."

Nolan eyeballs all the fancy work being done on my father's office and he wants to know how much this is going to set him back. Like he's some poverty case or something. Going on pure instinct and adrenalin, my father replies, cool as a cucumber: "I don't take a case unless I have a retainer of ten grand ($10,000)."

In today's dollars we're talking $100,000, so big, bad Nolan was more than shocked, and so he said to my father: "What in the hell do you think I did, kid? All I did is peddle a little booze; I didn't murder anyone!" Then, as he left in disgust, he added: "The hell with you!"

My poor father just stood there and wished he had only asked for three or four grand so he could pay the contractor, and just when he was wondering how he was going to explain all this to my mother, the big Irishman has a change of heart, walks back into the office with hat in hand and says: "Really, kid, could you really get me off?"

That's not a scene from a movie, that's a real chapter from my father's life, and my father replied without missing a beat: "I know I can get you off." Nolan was speechless. Then he reached into the pocket of that fancy, downtown suit of his, counts out a hundred, one-hundred dollar bills, and lays them on the carpenter's mat for my father to see. There it was in green-and-white: $10,000 in cash, and Nolan not only became my father's first client, but he made a good investment, because, of course, my father was as good as his word and got him off.

As to whether or not Nolan ever gave him one of those fancy $2 cigars he smoked, Dad never said.

But it is worth saying that my Italian-American father and his Irish-American partner, Joe Roach, were the go-to lawyers in Chicago for gangsters of both ethnic persuasions.

Dad started big, and with each success in the courtroom he became more powerful and sought-after. Maybe you've seen that movie called "Nitti, the Enforcer" (the Frank Nitti Story) that ABC runs occasionally. In it, there's a courtroom scene in which the judge looks up and says: "Mr. Parrillo, are you ready with your defense?"

That, I am proud to say, was a real slice from my father's life, because he really was Frank Nitti's defense attorney. And by 1940 my father had the political moxy and might to make Dwight Green

Governor of Illinois. Dwight Who, you say?

Many books refer to Dwight Green's prosecution of Al Capone when he was on trial in Chicago, but I will say it again without reservation: my dad, William Parrillo, made Dwight Green Governor of Illinois in 1940. And I promise to reveal all about this matter in a later chapter.

Northwestern University School of Law honored my father in 2003 by naming the William Parrillo Courtroom for his adept handling of a leading labor law case in 1934 before the United States Supreme Court. The case was called 'Meadowmoor Dairy vs. Chicago Milk Wagon Drivers Union.' It is still a leading labor law case, because it marked the first time a private enterprise got an injunction against a union. They knew they weren't going to break Meadowmoor, and their strikers were running out of money.

Dad's good deeds in Washington did not go unnoticed by what the FBI so famously dubbed "the Outfit" back in Chicago. And so when Prohibition ended, the Outfit expressed their gratitude for his legal brilliance by giving him the Meadowmoor Dairy on the near Westside of Chicago at 1334 South Peoria Street.

The Outfit gave Dad the dairy, but they kept the milk-hauling trucks which they had used during Prohibition to haul bootleg whiskey into the city and distribute it. After Prohibition, they obviously had other nefarious uses for those innocent looking trucks, but they had no use for the dairy itself.

So there was my father in 1934, the proud new

In 2003, Chicago's Northwestern University School of Law named
the Parrillo Courtroom in honor of Donnie's father, William Parrillo.
In 1934, the senior Parrillo masterfully argued the 'Meadowmoor
Dairy vs. Chicago Milk Wagon Drivers Union' before the Supreme
Court, a leading labor law case that still stands as of this writing.
(Rubloff Building, Room 155)

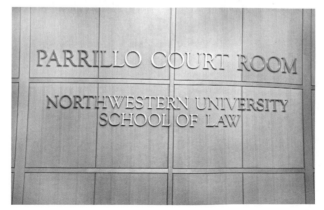

owner of a dairy that he decided would operate under a non-union status. That was a bold move on my father's part, because the Chicago Milk Wagon Drivers Union decided to call their first strike that same year. All the other dairies knuckled under and stopped producing milk, but Meadowmoor, under my dad, continued producing milk around the clock. And they were the only dairy that was producing milk for Chicago.

Enraged, the union had somebody throw a bomb into dad's dairy. Somebody. I never knew who-kicked the bomb out on the sidewalk.

The bomb detonated minutes later, blowing the doors off the dairy. The Chicago Fire Department refused to classify the incident as anything more than a common fire. I guess uncommon bomb throwings don't count. And the bombing proved that the union was just as violent as the companies they opposed. They didn't hesitate to use their goons and musclemen when and where they saw fit, and no one ever saw them in shining armor on white horses.

Anyway, things went from bad to worse with the kidnapping and subsequent murder of the head of the Chicago Milk Wagon Drivers Union. The Secretary/Treasurer of the union succeeded him, but he called off the strike after unknown assailants beat him with baseball bats.

I tell you, my father didn't practice law in some storybook kingdom by the sea. He was Taylor Street tough and, as you will see in the next chapter, that meant that he could keep his head while

Sue Bundesen and 52 in Milk Strike 'Plot'

As a sequel to the recent dairy strike which deprived Chicago of milk supply for three days, a suit was filed in federal court yesterday charging Dr. Herman N. Bundesen, president of the board of health, and fifty-two other individuals and firms, with conspiracy to fix prices and restrain trade.

The suit, filed in behalf of the Meadowmoor Dairies, Inc., and the Economy Dairy Company, Inc., seeks an injunction against all the defendants, and appointment of a receiver for all the dairy companies and affiliated firms named in the bill.

DISCUSS CRIMINAL ACTION.

Immediately after filing the suit, the five attorneys who represent the two complaining firms went before District Attorney Dwight Green and discussed with him the possibility of criminal action, growing out of the alleged conspiracy.

Mr. Green said the charges made in the bill would be turned over to investigators of the Department of Justice.

Numerous acts of violence during the recent milk strike are set forth, such as dumping milk trucks, halting trains and threatening violence to workers.

The Milk Strike - to read the full article please go to our website:
www.caponemaygofree.com

people around him were losing theirs, literally.

So one strike ends, but another begins - this time in 1937. Dad held out, because he had grown his little dairy into the largest wholesale operation in Chicago.

Those were the days before supermarkets - just "Ma & Pa" neighborhood stores, and Dad's Meadowmoor was selling them milk for 4 cents a quart, substantially cheaper than the prices offered by the union dairies. They couldn't compete, and they knew it, and that made them mighty sore.

So when the Meadowmoor bottles would go back to the bottle exchange, the other dairies would break them, depriving dad's company of their 2 cents per bottle deposit. That 2 cents was a lot of money for those housewives who would return their empty Meadowmoor bottles. Dad harnessed that housewife anger by having them stand on street corners holding signs that read: "I need milk for my babies."

He also had old people park their wheelchairs in front of hospitals and tell anyone who would listen that they would die if they didn't get their milk.

Dad didn't need some high-priced public relations firm to tell him how to turn the press and popular opinion in his favor. He stood strong, and he prevailed, and I only wish he had kept on prevailing for decades more.

The good often die young and that was certainly true for my father who never made it to 50. He suffered from asthma and the doctor had him on some new medicine, and it literally broke his heart. Like I said at the outset of this book, the anniversary of my father's death is always the darkest day of the year for me, and I have lived considerably past his 48 years.

Maybe you've seen that great Frank Capra movie they show every Christmas Eve called "It's a Wonderful Life." In the movie, the character played by Jimmy Stewart has to take over the Bailey Building & Loan after his father dies suddenly of a heart attack. Well, I had to do pretty much the same thing after my dad died of a heart attack by becoming Vice President of Meadowmoor Dairy after I was graduated from college at the tender age of 21.

My father was the one who made the company

famous, but I did coin a memorable phrase while I was at Meadowmoor: "You can't beat our milk, but you can whip our cream!"

But this chapter is about my father, not about me, and I do have to tell you that the Parrillo & Roach Law Firm handled cases all over the United States.

Even when they were not the Attorney-of-Record, they were the Attorney-in-Fact. And, yes, they were the most politically connected firm with major clients, who, in those days, had big incomes from what we might politely call "illicit rackets."

As I said, my father was Taylor Street tough, and, in the next chapter, I am going to tell you all about our "Little Italy" near the Chicago Loop.

It was truly a village unto itself, and it existed in a city full of ethnic enclaves where Irish, Jewish, and even German gangsters ruled their respective roosts. The Italians, of course, eventually triumphed over the other organizations, and the FBI gave them that famous, aforementioned code name which still stands today: "The Chicago Outfit."

Read all about that here in my book, and meet Marilyn Monroe and those low-down Kennedy brothers, Jack and Bobby, and their gangster father Joe, and all the rest, but before you turn out the light, I want to leave you with what I call:

A Little Side Story.

In 1939, my mother and father took my older brother and me to attend the World's Fair in New York City and we stayed at the world famous Waldorf-Astoria Hotel. And so one morning my

When Donnie's parents took him to the 1939 World's Fair in New York where he had the pleasure of meeting Mr. Frank Costello. He later learned Mr. Costello was one of the biggest crime bosses and bootleggers in New York City and a partner of Joe Kennedy.

mother took me and my brother to breakfast in the dining room, while my father met with a man at another table. My mother told me to go and tell my father that we had to leave right away so she could meet her girlfriend, Genevieve, in front of the General Motors Pavilion.

So I went over and said: "Dad, Mom says we have to go now."

And he said: "All right, just a few more minutes, and we'll leave."

I reported back to Mom, and she soon got antsy and said: "Go tell your dad we have to leave immediately."

As I started walking back to the other table, my father and the other man were just getting up, and so Dad said to me: "Say hello to Mr. Costello."

And I, in my infinite wisdom, thought I would be a wise-guy and refer to the famous comedy team of Abbott & Costello. So I shook his hand and said: "Hi, Mr. Costello. Where's Abbott?"

I thought I was quite the comedian until my father came to our table, grabbed me by the neck and said: "You ever talk that way to an adult again, and I'll ring your neck for you."

Turns out that my father was not talking to a member of the Abbott & Costello comedy team, but rather to Frank Costello himself who was one of the big bosses of the New York Crime Syndicate families and a partner of Ambassador Joe Kennedy in the bootlegging business.

Now please get a good night's sleep, because you've got lots of exciting reading yet to come.

Donnie Parrillo

CHAPTER TWO

THE OLD NEIGHBORHOOD
(A World of Our Own)

There are big years, and then there are big years, and 1930 had to be the biggest of them all, because it marked three great beginnings:

1. The Chicago Outfit

2. The Great Depression

3. Yours truly, one Donald "Donnie" Parrillo.

More about the first two in a bit, but for number three you need to know that I was born and raised in a "world of our own" within that melting pot of a city called Chicago.

Except we weren't allowed to melt in too much, because in my old Italian neighborhood just south west of the famous Loop, we were two things people didn't like in those days - Italian and Catholic.

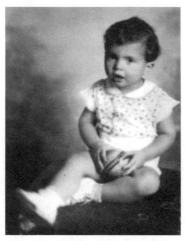

Donnie W. Parrillo as a toddler.

We're talking about Taylor Street here, and most of the kids I grew up with greeted the nuns in Italian the first day they went to school. And if they didn't greet Sister in Italian, they said "good morning" with a heavy Italian accent.

Fortunately, my parents were well-educated American, and my mother refused to ever teach us her native language for fear that we would develop Italian accents.

But, you know, when I listen to a Verdi opera, I am sorry I never learned Italian, because it is truly the language of the soul. And I wouldn't be surprised at all to get to heaven and hear the angels singing arias from Verdi and Puccini operas.

While the old Italian families in the Taylor Street neighborhood were not well educated, they were hard-working, salt-of-the-earth people. The kind of people you wanted to grow up with and have around you at all times.

When, for example, you walked into a neighbor's home, they immediately offered you food and drink. Didn't matter how poor they might be. You were their guest, and they made you feel welcome in that warm Italian manner.

Everyone in the old Taylor Street neighborhood worked hard and they all strived for what they considered the tastiest slice of the American dream-pie: a three-flat.

They would live on the first floor and rent out the second and third floors, and they would have arrived in "cielo," or heaven. And then, when the oldest child got married, they would give them the second floor flat, and they would give the third floor to the second child when he or she got married. And they would make a "garden apartment" in the basement for the third child and his new bride.

And for us Italian-Americans, the most important status symbol was a big, beautiful lamp placed right in the middle of the window for everyone to see.

You have to realize that those old-time Italians escaped oppression in Italy in search of freedom and the American dream. And most of them found it.

And in striving for that American dream, we closed ranks and formed a community that was so tightly knitted that on those rare occasions when an Irish family moved in, we'd say: "He'd better be a damned tough guy or a damned fast runner."

And there were the inevitable fights with the

Irish, with a big 200-pound Irish kid beating up a skinny little Italian kid with his fists and calling that a "fair fight." But then the next day the little Italian kid would retaliate with a baseball bat, and the battered and bruised Irish bully would call "foul" and say that "wasn't a fair fight."

But we eventually accepted the Irish, and, yes, some of those Irish kids brought pride to the neighborhood with their great athletic feats.

And speaking of sports, our number one pastime was 16-inch softball with no gloves, no catcher's mask, no nothing but your bare hands and a bat, and a whole lot of hustle. And if you jammed your fingers trying to catch a ball that was bigger and harder than a rock, everybody else would just hold up mangled fingers and give you the raspberries. Games would go on every single day after school and on weekends. And what great games they were. And just because the pitcher delivered the ball underhand and slow, don't think he didn't have his moves, and don't think he couldn't get you to swing early or late or just pop up to the short centerfielder. That's right. There's a short centerfielder in 16-inch softball.

It's a whole other game, and we played it for all it's worth in our old Chicago neighborhood. The other thing we would do on weekends would be to go the neighborhood movie theater and watch the serials and a double feature.

I especially remember Tom Mix up there on the silver screen riding his horse "Tony" to capture all the bad guys who, of course, were wearing black hats. Maybe I should have become a movie critic.

We had our movie theater and we had our own butcher, baker, drugstore, dry cleaner, and even our own police station.

It's like some giant lifted a village right out of Italy and plunked it down near downtown Chicago. The coppers walked the beat in those days, and our local policemen knew every kid in the neighborhood by name. That made for a safer, friendlier neighborhood, and I would humbly suggest that if more police officers would walk the beat today, we would have a whole lot less crime. But that's just my humble opinion.

When I was growing up in the old Taylor Street neighborhood, the Great Depression was in full force. When people couldn't find work, friends and neighbors would lend a hand, and you could walk into any home in our "village" and have as good a meal as you would find in the fanciest restaurant in Chicago.

And everything was homemade and cooked with love, from the sausage and bread to the pasta. Ever try to make pasta at home? Not easy, is it? Well, making pasta at home just came naturally in a neighborhood where the older folks set the example by treating others with a distinct respect and friendship.

They all came from hard times and really wanted their children and grandchildren to have a better life here in America. And so it was no surprise that my little neighborhood produced a disproportionate number of doctors, lawyers, scientists, and college professors. And, yes, a few bad apples, who you will meet shortly.

On warm nights, we'd all gather at the corner of Taylor and Oakley in front of the drugstore. There might be as many as 30 of us, and none of us had two nickels to rub together or the means to travel outside the neighborhood. So we'd just congregate at that storied old corner and shoot the bull, argue about sports, critique the movies we had just seen, and, of course, practice our wolf whistles on passing beauties who would keep on going, just to tease us. And that certainly hasn't changed, but don't get me started.

Anyway, the meeting on the corner would start to break up around 10 p.m., and everybody would head for home, but every once in a while you would hear guns shots. And you wouldn't know until the next day who had been killed. You see the younger Italians were more restless and dissatisfied than their parents and grandparents.

The older generation just wanted to live in peace and quiet, but the younger crowd was hungry for power and money, and they aspired to be like those flashy gangsters from the area who drove the best cars and wore the finest clothes.

Today kids want to be like those celebrity movie stars and sports stars, but back then kids in our neighborhood just wanted to be a successful criminal who drove beautiful dames around in the biggest car money could buy.

That was success. And I'll never forget two of our aspiring gangsters who came to bad ends.

WEDNESDAY, OCTOBER

LITTLE ITALY'S' TOUCH IS FOUND ALL OVER CHICAGO

Doctors, Lawyers, Merchants, Chiefs, Judges, Manufacturers; Every Phase of Life Here Has Successful Figures.

A series of articles on the achievements of the Jewish race in Chicago, written by Dr. G. George Fox, starts in tomorow's Herald and Examiner.

Chicago—the world's greatest melting pot!
There are in this city today no fewer than 450,000 Germans, 400,-
000 Poles, 300,000 Jews, 300,000 Irish, 200,000 Italians, 200,000 Bohem-
ians and Czecho-Slovaks, 125,000 Swedes, 50,000 Norwegians and 50,-
000 Greeks, including both foreign and native born of each nationality.
The Herald and Examiner has asked an outstanding leader of a
number of the principal nationalities here to write a series of special
articles about the contribution of his own race to the development of
Chicago. These articles appear daily in this newspaper.

BY JUDGE FRANCIS BORRELLI,

A Leading Municipal Court Jurist and Himself a Product of "Little Italy."

Law, medicine, engineering, politics, commerce, manu-facturing—

In all of those fields, leaders of Italian extraction are carving out names for themselves.

To read the full article go to our website: www.caponemaygofree.com and click on the link for News Clippings.

One we called "Bull" because he was a big, rough, tough guy, and we called his partner in crime, "Italo." Why, I don't remember, but I do know Italo was the tallest, skinniest Italian I have ever seen. So one night Bull and Italo went over to Humboldt Park, which was northwest of us, and robbed the box office of the Oval where they had these popular six-day bicycle races. Bull and Italo figured that with all the people who went to see these races all the time, the box office had to be over-flowing with cash. But all they got for their troubles was $275, and a policeman who happened to be guarding the box office. Bull popped him, and the officer died with Italo, the accomplice, looking on.

The entire Chicago Police Department came down on those two would-be gangsters, and Bull was given a one-way ticket to the electric chair within 30 days of his guilty sentence for first-degree murder.

They didn't mess around in those days, as Bull found out the hard way. As for Italo, he ended up serving 14 years of a 20-year sentence for being an accomplice to murder.

So we produced the doctors and lawyers and scientists, and occasionally a few bad apples like Bull and Italo rolled out of our barrel.

And that leads me to the murder of Blackie Sullivan. Blackie was a professional thief who frequented saloons in the neighborhood where he would become a mean drunk.

And one night Blackie was having more than his share of drinks in just such a saloon when he got into an argument with a guy from our neighborhood. So the owner of the tavern flipped a gun to our guy, and he shot Blackie Sullivan, point blank.

Thinking on their feet, the other patrons dragged what they thought was Blackie's still warm body out on the street so the tavern owner wouldn't lose his liquor license.

The police happened to come by about that time, and saw Blackie Sullivan lying on the street with blood coming out of him, and, seeing that he was still alive, they rushed him to the hospital.

True story.

And while Blackie is recovering in the hospital, he starts chirping like a chickadee about how he's going to "settle up" with that guy from Polk and Oakley who plugged him at the saloon.

So Blackie finally recovers after a couple of months, and just as a couple of his confederates are coming to pick him up from the hospital, this car roars up and somebody shoots Blackie a second time.

Well, what better place to be shot than the entrance to a hospital, and they rush him back in and patch him up a second time. Another month passes, and a shot-up Blackie Sullivan is back on the street, and he's just getting into his car when an unknown shooter sneaks up and blows his head off with a shotgun.

It's a done deal-Blackie Sullivan is finally dead, once and for all. He got, as we say, "Taylor Street Justice." And nobody ever traced this crime to Taylor Street, and nobody ever said a word about who the shooter was, even though we all knew who he was. And so that was the end of a mean drunk named Blackie Sullivan who never had any business being in our old neighborhood.

But enough of Blackie Sullivan and back to our games of good, old 16-inch softball. Yeah, the ball for night games was yellow, not white like it was for day games, and it looked like a small cantaloupe, and it hurt like the devil when you caught it the wrong way with your bare hands, but that didn't stop us from having some great games.

And we played most of our ball games at the corner of Polk and Oakley on a cinder lot that was about as far from the "friendly confines" of Wrigley Field as you could get. Meaning that sometimes you'd be sliding into a base and pick up a load of cinders that would stay in your leg for a week.

You had to be tough to play 16-inch softball in the old neighborhood, especially when the inevitable fist fights broke out over who was safe or who was out. We settled such disputes with some good, old-fashioned "pow-pow" to the jaw or the belly.

But as rough and tumble as we were on that old cinder ball field of ours, we would stop playing every time a nun or a priest passed by. And three of those kids I played with went to the electric chair when they got older.

We were tough kids, but we respected our nuns and priests enough to call time-out when they passed by. And we never thought of picking up the bat and ball on Good Friday, even though we were sorely tempted.

We called our team "The Unknowns," and I was known at short as "Luscious Luke" for my obvious resemblance to the White Sox's ace shortstop,

Lucius "Luke" Appling.

Well, maybe I never played short for the Sox, but my middle name was Lucius, so they called me Luscious Luke whenever I took the field for The Unknowns, and we took to fields all over Chicago, because 16-inch softball was the biggest thing going in the Windy City at that time. They even had a Windy City League that played their games under the lights at night at St. Phillips Stadium at Van Buren and Kedzie.

My father sponsored a team called the William Parrillo Boosters. Dad was a prominent politician, and he wanted to get his name out there, and what better venue than the most popular sport at that time, 16-inch softball. And the Boosters delivered for Dad by winning the title two or three years in a row.

And one year they played "The Witt Handley Yankees" for the league championship, and there was a lot of money riding on that game, because Witt Handley was a well-known labor leader in Chicago.

So on the night before the big game, people in our neighborhood found some Witt Handley Yankees and subtly suggested that it might be in their best interests to call in sick before the game. If you know what I mean.

That little bit of persuasion worked, because only four of their regular players showed up to play, and they had to complete their line-up with people in the stands who didn't know the difference between and bat and a ball.

So anyone who just happened to bet on the Parrillo Boosters came up big that night.

That's the way it was in our neighborhood, and that brings us to a colorful politician named "Diamond Joe" Esposito who lived right across the street from our cinder ballpark at Polk and Oakley. One Sunday afternoon, Diamond Joe was at the drugstore on that corner with his bodyguard, Joe Varshetto. All's well as they started walking home, but Varshetto didn't see Diamond Joe safely to his door, because the bodyguard lived in the middle of a long block, and he figured his boss could make it safely the rest of the way, about 100 yards.

Bad move, because after Varshetto went into his house, a car pulled up next to the defenseless Diamond Joe, and two shooters emptied their "Tommy Guns" into Diamond Joe, riddling him with machine gun bullets.

He was dead before he hit the sidewalk there about the middle of the block on Oakley. That was right where we played on a porch, and that porch and building were riddled with bullet holes. That building was a historic landmark for us until it was torn down.

And then a week after Diamond Joe met his untimely end on Oakley, another Taylor Street character called "the Bomber" was shot by a Melrose Park man known as "Tony the Ghost." He got Taylor Street Justice.

Life was never dull in the old neighborhood, and as Tony the Ghost was busy "whacking" the

Bomber, the Bomber's sister jumped on his body. She got shot for her troubles, but that didn't bother Tony the Ghost, who got in his car and fled to parts unknown.

That all tied back to the killing of Diamond Joe, because everyone said the Bomber was the one who finally finished the job on Diamond Joe Esposito with a shotgun.

As for the Bomber, why he died of what we Italians would consider "unnatural causes" - a heart attack, not Taylor Street Justice. Go figure. And you have to figure that those weren't the only killings in our quiet little neighborhood just south-west of downtown Chicago.

One young thief would pop his partner in crime when they couldn't settle on a split, and, really, that was no different than what you see happening in Black and Hispanic neighborhoods today. I feel their pain, because I lived it when I was growing up on Taylor Street.

And don't think we didn't have contact with kids in the Black neighborhoods back then. We were way ahead of the times, because we booked softball games in Black neighborhoods where there were some mighty fine ball players. And just to prove that point, one of their teams beat us three games in a row. They creamed us, so we mixed sides for the fourth game, with five blacks and five whites on each team. Remember that in softball you have 10 players what with that short center to fill in that gap where most of the pop-ups were hit. So I went home that night and told my Dad:

"You know, when I played on the team today, we had five black players and five white players."

My father gave me a look I'll never forget and said: "No, I don't want to hear anything like that. You had on your team 10 baseball players."

My father taught me a lesson in color-blindness that serves me well to this day, and, if you could see me in church on Sunday, you would really know just how color-blind I really am. And I owe it all to my father, William Parrillo.

Thanks, Dad!

And thanks, Mom and Dad, for raising me in a neighborhood in which our entire social life centered around our parish church, St. Callistus.

We went to one another's First Communions and Confirmations, and we loved to go to church breakfasts. The highlight of the year was the "Feast" which made the most money for our poor parish. But St. Callistus did just fine, because after you put your money in the bucket on Sunday, the ushers would pass another bucket to make you pay ten cents "rent" for your seat in the pew.

All year long, the priests would tell us that it's illegal and immoral to gamble, but when that famous Feast came along for its five-day run, they would allow the Outfit to operate a little roulette, craps, and blackjack for the good of the parish.

And there was no outside catering in those days, because the women would cook and serve the food, which was better than you can even imagine, and, yes, prohibition was over so there was liquor, which was provided by the Outfit. And they thoughtfully split the proceeds with the church. They always gave the church the right count, and that made the priests happy because it meant that the church had enough money to continue on for another year.

Like I said, the food at the St. Callistus Feast was better than anything you could find at the best restaurant in Chicago, and it was all home cooked Italian food prepared by excellent cooks.

But the women didn't mind doing all that cooking for the church, because their social lives centered on St. Collistus Church. On Thursday, a bunch of them would go to church for choir practice, and on Saturday, another bunch of them would scrub the church from top to bottom in preparation for Sunday. Then on Monday, the women would go back to church and clean up after Sunday Mass.

That same level of care and concern carried over into all aspects of our lives in the neighborhood. So when someone got sick, he or she would have 'round-the-clock' care from the neighbors. They would nurse their neighbor 24-hours a day until they were fully recovered. I tell you, when they talk on the news about the sorry state of our health care system, I always look back to the way things were in the old neighborhood and think, now, there's a model health care system for the whole country. Would be nice, wouldn't it, if we all cared for one another the way we did back on Taylor Street in the old days?

But the camaraderie we had in the Old Neighborhood is probably something we'll never have again. That's a pity, because now everyone goes to the government for whatever help they need.

But in the old days, which were really the good, old days, you relied on your friends and neighbors, not some government bureaucrat - for food, shelter, medical attention, whatever you needed. And although we had our own police station and the coppers walked the beat and knew us kids by name, we kept to the code of "silence" whenever anything went wrong.

So when the police came asking questions, the answer was always: "Nobody heard anything, and nobody saw anything."

We had our own system of justice, and it served us just fine, thank you very much. And we knew how to respond when somebody died.

You waked the deceased in the living room of their homes, sometimes for as long as two weeks. And during the wake, all the women in the neighborhood would dress entirely in black and bring on the food, and keep bringing on the food.

There's nothing like it today, and that is truly a shame, because that was the caring and civilized way in which to respond to the death of a beloved member of the community. Sure, it was a social occasion for the whole neighborhood, but even we children were part of it, because if a member of your family died, you would wear a black armband in his honor for a whole year. A whole year!

And during that mourning period, you couldn't go to the movies or play softball. We respected our dead, and we sacrificed the things we loved for them. But it wasn't all tears and sorrow, because there was all that great food and fellowship.

Yes, we would gather to mourn our deceased neighbor, but we would mix laughter with the tears as we recalled colorful episodes from his or her life. And the deceased was never alone, because five or six women would stand watch by his or her side every night until the funeral and shed real tears.

So what about the Italian men? What was their social life? In a word: bocce.

Bocce is an Italian game played with a little ball called the Pauline, and the big ball with stripes and plains that you have to roll close to the Pauline to score. It is truly a game of concentration and skill, and on Sunday afternoons in the old neighborhood you would see 20 games going on.

And the best way to play bocce was with a good cigar, and a bottle of wine and all that great Italian food that their wives would bring over. Okay, you probably took in more calories than you burned off while playing bocce, but those games were as close to heaven, or 'cielo,' as the men in my neighborhood could get in this life. Sadly, that camaraderie and friendship is a thing of the past.

We live in a totally different era today and gladly tolerate government interference in every aspect of our lives. Whether that's good or bad is anyone's opinion, but I know to this day that when one of my old friends from the Old Neighborhood dies, all of us who are still here show up at the funeral parlor.

We reminisce for hours about our life and times

together in the neighborhood. And what times they were. And what a mostly pleasant picture I have painted so far of the Old Neighborhood.

It was sunny and pleasant all right, and the food was wonderful, and our softball games were the best, but there was a darker side to the neighborhood, and that was best expressed by the "Made Man" from the Outfit who had the life-and-death authority of one of those dukes from our Italian city states.

A Made Man, of course, was a man chosen as a member by the Outfit and duly initiated in a ritual so secret no one has lived to tell about it, and our Made Man was none other than "Big Frank" Rio, or simply "Frankie R."

When you had a dispute with your neighbor you both went to Big Frank, and, like King Solomon from the Bible, he would listen to both sides, and then he would make a wise decision, one way or the other. He was just like an elected judge, except that you could not appeal a decision by Big Frank. It was final, like it or not.

So that was the dark side to our Old Neighborhood, but it was also a bright side, because having a Made Man in charge made for a much safer neighborhood with rules that were better than the ones written in stone, because they were written in blood.

If, for example, you decided to rape a neighborhood girl, you would not live long enough to rape a second neighborhood girl. That meant that the girls and women could walk around the neighborhood at night without worry. How many neighborhoods do you know like that today?

And there was a hard-and-fast rule for our professional burglars: "Go to another neighborhood and rob. Or else." And nobody wanted to find out what the "or else" meant. And I came to appreciate what our Old Neighborhood really meant when we moved to a western suburb when I was 15.

Dad was really doing well at that time, and we lived in a big, beautiful home with maids and chauffeurs. Sounds swell, doesn't it?

Well, let me tell you: I hardly ever said hello to any of the neighbors, and I didn't even know their first names, just their last names. At school, the other kids wore clothes I had never seen before back in the Old Neighborhood - white buckskin shoes, yellow corduroy pants and Argyle sweaters.

And if that wasn't enough, suddenly there were girls in school. That was a big shock for me, because I had just come from a Catholic school in which boys and girls were separated. So it was a shock for me all right, but I adjusted just fine, and, you know, I really came to like having girls in class with me. But I still missed the camaraderie I enjoyed in the Old Neighborhood, because there was nothing like it in the suburbs.

I continued missing it so much that I returned to the Old Neighborhood 17 years after moving away to be elected Alderman of the famous First Ward of Chicago. And you will read all about it later in this book, but I have to tell you right now that when I returned to Taylor Street I found that most of my old friends were still living there.

And I think they were happier to see me get elected alderman than I was. They all congratulated me, and I still have the letters that many of them wrote to me at the time. So while I was serving as their Alderman, I never missed a wake, and I would go to every funeral I could.

Even today I still stop by old St. Callistus Catholic Church where I had my first communion and was confirmed. Sadly, the old priests are all gone, but I can still hear them saying the Mass in Latin, and I remember sitting in that old church as a kid and thinking: "Boy, this is a big church!"

Now, when I go there for a funeral or a wedding, it looks like a little cracker box. And I feel sad because the paint is peeling off the walls, the radiators are all exposed, and the pews are hard as rocks. But being there reminds me of when I was inside that old church passing out political literature, or going to the parish breakfast with my mother, who was very active in the church.

Oh, and here's a fun fact about my old church: it was named for a Roman slave who was put in charge of a bank who was elected Pope in 217 - Callistus I.

Remember how I said that the police walked the beat in our Old Neighborhood? Well, when one of "our" policemen caught you doing something wrong, he would walk you right back home and tell your parents what you had done.

I would rather he had taken me to the police

station for a night in jail, because when he brought
me home, off came my father's belt. I'd be over his
knee in a second, and he'd paddle me so good I
couldn't sit for days.

We respected our beat coppers, and we were
more afraid of them taking us home than locking
us up. And we had a great rapport with them, and,
sure, they'd put up with a lot of our pranks so long
as we didn't seriously violate the law. When we did
that, it was straight home to Dad and his belt!

And that brings me to the big question: Who's
better off? People in our "modern" society with
government looking over our shoulders every second of the day, or the people in our Old Neighborhood who didn't have much in the way of material
pleasures, but had all the love and warmth you
could ever ask for?

You know the answer, and so do I: the people
in the Old Neighborhood were better off than we
are today, because they didn't look to the government to solve their problems. They solved their
problems themselves, and they had the Made Man
from the Outfit to act as the court of final appeal.

Today we're forever talking about day care for
children, but in the old days the women of the
neighborhood would look after one another's kids.
And I'd be rich if I had a nickel for every spanking
I got from another kid's mom. Not only would she
spank me, but she would keep me under "house
arrest" in her house until my parents got home, and
she'd tell them what I did, and, of course, I'd get
another spanking. It's a wonder I can still sit in one

place for more than five minutes. I tell you.

Today, you see kids talking back to adults all the time, but you never saw that in our Old Neighborhood, because we respected our elders. Sometimes I wish I could teleport today's kids back to old Taylor Street for a few days of "boot camp." They'd come back to the present with a whole lot better attitude, that's for sure.

The Old Neighborhood will always be part of me, and I will never forgot those experiences and people who made me who I am.

Taylor Street was my salt, and it truly made me "a man for all seasons." That meant that a man from our neighborhood was comfortable in any world in which he found himself.

He could have lunch downtown with the head of the First National Bank and talk wisely of business and finance and use all the right knives and forks, and head back to Taylor Street that afternoon for a hot game of craps in the alley.

I know my Taylor Street education made me equally comfortable in both of those worlds. So little wonder that I ended up owning a national bank at the tender age of 32.

You would have to say I was lucky, because when I was a kid in the Old Neighborhood, I only knew that banks were where the rich people kept their money. People like us only went to banks to rob the rich people's loot. So imagine me owning a bank at the age of 32. I certainly could not have imagined it when I was a kid.

Finally, let's have a little fun with names,

specifically with nicknames. Everyone in the Old Neighborhood had one, and it got so as you didn't really know anyone's real name. Maybe the priest did, but we sure didn't.

So I want to close this chapter with a glossary of some of our more memorable nicknames. Don't worry; there's not going to be a test or anything, but I just thought you might like to know how we came up with such colorful nicknames and how and why we applied them to one another. Sometimes it was given in hate, and sometimes it was applied love and kindness, but it always fit.

And you wore your nickname with honor, and when it came time to leave the Old Neighborhood, you had three words emblazoned on your heart:

LOYALTY

HONOR

RESPECT

Yes, it was truly a world of our own, and here's that glossary straight from that wonderful world.

The RUBBISH PILE - after Taylor Street Justice had been meted out, bodies were then found on rubbish piles behind buildings or homes.

- A body found on a rubbish pile was considered garbage.

- A body found on a rubbish pile with a penny or a nickel in his hand meant he stole small change.

- A body found on the rubbish pile with his hand cut off meant he got it caught in the cash register.

- A body found on the rubbish pile with his tongue cut out meant that he talked too much.

- A body found on the rubbish pile with the throat cut meant he talked to the "G," or government.

- And, of course, a body with his penis cut off meant he raped the wrong girl.

NICKNAMES from the Old Neighborhood:

- Jelly Belly: He had the biggest book showing on Grand Avenue.

- Big Frank Rio: He was the "Made Man" in the Old Neighborhood.

- Jimmy Army: A bookmaker in Cicero with no left arm.

- Lefty: A bookmaker with no right arm.

- Leggy: A guy with no left leg.

- Mousy: A little guy who used to run around collecting bets.

- Dr. Teets: The old man who ran the card game at Grand and May where the local police would go in and collect the payoff every day.

- Crippled Gus: He was in a wheelchair all his life.

- Kreepy Karpus: The son of Alvin Karpus who was killed by J. Edgar Hoover.

- Sweet Willie: A jewelry fence.

- Willie Potatoes: A Made Man.

- Needles: A Made Man.

- Kracky (short for Krackers): A Made Man.

- Curley: He had a big mop of hair.

- Baldy: He was totally bald.

- Diamond Joe: The politician gunned down in our Old Neighborhood.

- Jimmy the Bomber: Suspected to be Diamond Joe's killer.

- Haircuts: Our local barber.

- Cakes: His family owned a bakery that made most of the wedding cakes in the neighborhood.

- The Strangler: He was accused of strangling a man, but he was never convicted.

- Whacked: Killed. As in: "He got Taylor Street Justice."

- Hit: Murder. Again: "Taylor Street Justice."

- "G": The government.

- Sheenie Albert: An Italian who ran a book joint at Van Buren and Western.

- Benny the Book: The over-dressed Jew who ran a book joint out of the Roosevelt Coffee Shop at Roosevelt and Halsted.

- Joe D: the Made Man who ran the Rush Street area.

CHAPTER THREE

AL CAPONE ARRIVES
(MAKING OF A KING)

Al Capone arrived in Chicago in 1921.

I repeat: Al Capone arrived in Chicago in 1921, and his timing could not have been better, because that toddlin' town of Chicago was reeling from the effects of Prohibition.

The Windy City was thus set for the cigar-chomping son of a poor barber from Brooklyn, New York who was brought to Chicago by John Torrio to add some real muscle to his operation.

Torrio, you see, was part of "Big Jim" Colosimo's little crew, and he was looking to move up in the organization. Enter Al Capone, and the word still is that Torrio had Capone gun Colosimo down in the foyer of his restaurant.

The rap never got pinned on Capone, but the word is still out there that Big Al made his Chicago debut in a very splashy manner.

So, we have the son of a poor Brooklyn barber in Chicago, and it wasn't long before Capone and Torrio were peddling illegal whiskey. Hey, the government created a perfect business opportunity by passing Prohibition right after World War I when all those thirsty doughboys were coming home from the "War to End All Wars."

But Capone and Torrio weren't the only ones seeking to make their fortunes from the distribution and sale of bootleg whiskey. Those "made men" I talked about in the last chapter were very much in control of whiskey sales in much of Chicago, and they were none too happy to see a couple of greenhorns try to muscle in on their business.

So it was strictly business one night in the "Roaring Twenties" when John Torrio was walking into his house with his wife, and an "unknown assailant" jumped out of a car and put a bullet in his neck. That didn't kill Torrio, so the shooter tried to plug him with another while Torrio was bleeding on the ground in front of his hysterical wife. But, wouldn't you know, the shooter wasn't such a pro after all, because his gun jammed, and he was forced to scram out of there in the get-away car.

Turns out that the shooting was tied to the head of a union that Torrio and Capone were trying to take over, and that the man who tried to whack Torrio was himself killed a week later.

He got Taylor Street Justice.

Justice.

Chicago style.

Gone Are the Days ❧ **Whe**

MUST GO AS TOO ILLEGAL

$50,000 BREW TANK GOES FOR JUNK
Robert W. Dukelow (left) and La Verne | United States district attorneys, see Terry
Norris and William Parrillo, assistant | Druggan's old brewery destroyed.

Donnie's father, William Parrillo is noted above right and below left.

HOUSEHOLD STILL DEMONSTRATED BEFORE FEDERAL COMMISSIONER.
In left foreground: William Parrillo, assistant district attorney (left), and David Stansbury,
attorney for Jacob Lebed. Seated at right: John Smith, prohibition agent, who is testi-
fying, and Commissioner James R. Glass. The still is on the bench.

And the style of Chicago's organized crime scene at that time was that Italian and Irish gangs controlled the local rackets. But they weren't unified or coordinated, so the Italian leaders all got together and decided to organize as one big outfit. And whom should they pick to lead them, but that son of a poor barber from Brooklyn, New York: Al Capone.

He certainly must have impressed them all, because Capone wasn't even a "made man" at the time. But Capone knew how to organize crime, and he had them all agree to pool a portion of their profits every month for the good of all, and as a means for stopping the killing among them.

Capone took control of an organization that loomed larger in legend than in reality. And one of the accepted myths was that Bugsy Siegel started Las Vegas, Nevada, just like in that movie with Warren Beatty.

Let me tell you, when Siegel got to Vegas, he didn't find an empty stretch of desert, he found four hotels on a street that they were already calling "the Strip." And don't believe what you see in the movies, because Bugsy Siegel was killed in Los Angeles by the Chicago Crime Syndicate, not, as myth has it, because he robbed money from the Flamingo Hotel. And don't think you won't read a lot more about Bugsy and Las Vegas, because I am already planning to write a book about it!

So everybody agreed that Al Capone was the man for the job of organizing Chicago crime. He was a New Yorker with no local affiliations, and he did not have the big income of the other bosses. Plus, nobody else wanted to be the Boss then, or even later.

Well, there was Sam Giancana who truly wanted to be Boss, and we'll get to him shortly, but right now, you need to know that the top job was Capone's for the taking. Especially since it was considered a one-way ticket to a long stretch in the "big house." But that didn't stop Capone from becoming Boss.

And who were his troops? Well, in the last chapter you read all about my old Taylor Street neighborhood where "made men" made the law of the streets from Halsted Street to Western Avenue.

The five Genna brothers came to rule Taylor Street, but then Angelo Genna got killed, and a second brother met an untimely end at the hands of the Mob. A third Genna brother was shooting it out with other gangsters on Western Avenue when the police joined the fray and killed him.

Seeing the handwriting on the wall, the surviving two Genna brothers high-tailed it back to Italy and were never heard from again.

The territory west of Ashland Avenue was controlled by Frank Rio, who you read about in chapter 2. He was such a low-key gangster that the newspapers never really discovered him, and he died a natural death in 1935. He was one of the rare ones, that Frank Rio.

Moving west of Western at that time you entered the domain of the Irish gangs. They were as tough as they come, and "Terrible Tommy" Touhy (from chapter 1) and his brother Roger ruled the northwest suburbs with iron hands.

How terrible were they?

Well, Roger Touhy served 25 years in Stateville Penitentiary for kidnapping John "Jake the Barber" Factor. And he had only been out of Stateville for a couple of weeks when the Outfit whacked him while he was walking up the stairs to his sister's place on the near West Side.

Two police officers assigned to the Chicago Park District responded to the call even though they were only supposed to patrol boulevards and parks.

They shined a light in the eyes of the fallen Touhy, and one of the coppers asked: "Are you Roger Touhy?"

And that dying Irish gangster says to him: "Mind your own business, copper."

They rushed Touhy to St. Ann's Hospital on the northwest side, and doctors told Touhy they couldn't stop the bleeding and that he was going to die and that he should tell the police who shot him.

A copper then leaned over and asked: "Tell us who shot you, Roger?"

And Roger Touhy says to the two policemen at his side, Robert Louis and John O'Connor, "Go screw yourselves, coppers."

He died an hour later without snitching. So that was the colorful West Side.

And there on the even more colorful South

Side, in the fabled First Ward, you had an Italian enclave in Chinatown run by the Roti family. They dealt mainly with bootleg beer, not whiskey. And then south of 31st Street, you had "Dingbat" Oberta and "Pollock" Joe Salis. Frank McErlane, who even the Outfit respected, ran the show just south of Oberta and Salis, and "Klondyke" O'Donnell controlled everything down to the southern city limits. And then you had Chicago Heights, which was the strongest bastion of Italian power in the entire Chicago area, and which had as its "Roman Emperor," one Frank LaPorte.

People think Cicero was the center of Italian power in Chicagoland, but it was always Chicago Heights, which was almost 100 percent Italian. Cicero was mostly Czech, Polish, and Bohemian, and they didn't really control the city fathers there. They just kept paying them off.

Now things get really interesting as we go to the North Side of Chicago where the turf was being contested by the Dion O'Bannon Mob, and the Bugs Moran Mob. And if you were thinking that Bugs Moran was as Irish as Paddy's Pig, then you should know he was really Polish and probably spilled more kielbasa and sauerkraut than you ever ate.

O'Bannon and Moran also had to compete for control of the North Side with a confederation of Irish and German gangsters ruled by the Goosenburg Brothers, who entrusted the "business of eliminating the competition" to the straight-shooting Schemer Drucci.

And speaking of Schemer Drucci, Chicago Police Lieutenant Dan Healy and two of his officers told Schemer Drucci they were taking him to the station at 11th and State for questioning. Healy and his man must not have had a good road map, because they somehow ended up in the dingy domain of Lower Wacker Drive where Schemer Drucci got a good taste of his own medicine.

The coppers told the newspapers that Drucci, while in handcuffs, had grabbed Lieutenant Healy's gun and accidentally shot himself with it. If you believe that, I've got some islands in Lake Michigan I'd like to sell you.

No, what really happened is that the Outfit had it in for Drucci who had killed some of their guys, and they were not in the least reluctant to employ the "good" services of certain "crooked" members of the Chicago Police Department.

So that was the Chicago crime scene that greeted Al Capone when he arrived in 1921. Capone started small with just an area south of the Loop to 22nd Street, and his two partners in crime were Jake "Greasy Thumb" Guzik and Murray "the Camel" Humphrey. And everybody thought that Capone was the big Boss of Cicero too, but Louis "Little New York/Lefty" Campagna was king of Cicero.

When Campagna died, control of Cicero went to Joey "the Doves" Aiupa; Claude Maddox, who was also known as Johnny Moore; and Bobby Ansalme, who liked to call himself Bobby Jones for the famous golfer.

Joey Aiupa, you should know, was later sentenced to 29 years in prison for skimming money from Las Vegas casinos. They let him out when he was very ill, and he died shortly thereafter. And both Claude Maddox and Bobby Ansalme died of natural causes.

Meanwhile Al Capone was building his empire by filling his treasury with proceeds from all the gangs he controlled. But he achieved true stardom when he became the first to organize the Italian mobs, which were loosely organized. Like the city states of the old country, they were feuding with each other all the time over territory and treasure. So not all of them were funneling money up to Capone at the top. But Capone did have the respect and trust of all the other people. And, as my father would tell me later, his word was always 100 percent good, and people had total confidence in him. I never met Al Capone in person, but I certainly knew him through my father, who always respected his client's intelligence. Dad said Capone would have been a big man no matter what line of work he went into, and that he had a tremendous personality and loved to share jokes and laughter with people. And he was always impeccably groomed. Just look at his picture on the cover of this book. That says it all.

Al Capone stood about 5'10" and weighed 220 pounds, and my Dad said he was "all muscle." Too bad the NFL wasn't around in those day; he might have been one heck of a fullback.

Capone not only earned people's respect, but he

had a genius for organizing them into territories and working out profit-sharing plans that pleased his "people." But there were plenty of "people" at that time who operated outside Capone's control, and they were hell-bent in cutting in on his bootlegging enterprise.

So Capone didn't just walk into Chicago and take total control, and he had his weaknesses, number one of which was his love of the limelight. He loved it when his name hit the headlines and when people said "Capone is the most powerful man in Chicago."

If anybody believed in his own PR, it was Al Capone.

Al Capone loved the limelight, but he also worked steadily to organize crime in Chicago and to bring his fellow Italians together into one, big happy outfit. All that stood in the way of this new Roman Empire of the Midwest were the Irish and their gangs.

They were not going to roll over and play dead, not with all the money to be made on bootleg liquor. So a battle royal was brewing. But Capone also had to worry about the United States District Attorney who was out to put a feather in his cap called "Al Capone."

And the Government figured the best way to net Capone was to nail him on a net-worth income tax fraud case. They were so hot to get Capone that they claimed he was making $209 million a year. My Dad told me that Capone's income was probably more like $700,000 to $1 million a year.

So pour into this volatile mix the famous events of February 14, 1929: aka, the St. Valentine's Day Massacre. That was when seven members of Bugs Moran's North Side Gang were gunned down in a garage on North Clark Street. You walk past that spot today and all you see is an innocuous apartment building. But it was bloody hell on St. Valentine's Day 1929.

The St. Valentine's Day Massacre made Al Capone both a national and an international figure. He was larger than any local headline, and he remains an icon for organized crime. You say the name "Al Capone" to some kid in Beirut or Baghdad and he is going to make like a tommy gun. He might not know who the leader of his own country is, but he certainly will know all about Al Capone and the St. Valentine's Day Massacre.

But despite all his notoriety, Al Capone never became as powerful as the Outfit would become from the 1940s to the 1960s when it was totally organized.

And, wouldn't you know, when the St. Valentine's Day Massacre occurred on that miserable winter's day in Chicago, Capone was peacefully sunning himself at his Florida home.

And speaking of that home, I did spend some vacations there when I was 5 or 6, but Capone wasn't there. No, he was in the penitentiary, because the feds had finally caught up with him, but his brother, Ralph "Bottles" Capone, was there, and so I got to meet one member of the famous Capone family.

And, so you know, Bottles Capone died in 1978.

So, getting back to the fledgling Outfit when Capone was bringing the various Italian gangs together. The money was flowing faster and the future looked bright until two disasters struck:

1. President Roosevelt repealed Prohibition in 1933.

2. Al Capone was indicted for income tax evasion.

Talk about a double-whammy to the Outfit.

Anyway, in those days, hardly anybody ever filed income taxes. And nobody really had since income tax originated in 1913 when the total tax on your income was one-sixteenth of one percent.

So failing to file income tax was like getting a parking ticket - no big deal. No big deal unless you were an internationally known crime figure like Al Capone. Then it was a very, very big deal, because on the day before Capone's trial was to begin, Judge Wilkerson dismissed the entire jury and brought in another jury from another courtroom.

The newspapers said the judge switched juries, because Capone and his henchmen had bribed the original jurors and threatened to kill their families if they didn't provide an innocent verdict.

Dad told me that was pure hogwash. In fact, people were telling Capone to plead guilty, because the worst that could happen would be a piddly 60 or 90 day sentence. Capone would be out in no

ALTERIE LIED FOR CAPONE, CHARGE

As Louis ("Two Gun") Al-
terie, picturesque henchman of
Dean O'Banion in the early
days of Chicago gang warfare,
was arraigned before U. S.
Commissioner Edwin K.
Walker today on a charge of
perjury, it was disclosed that
the charge grew out of alleged
misstatements which he made
to the government in connection with a recent investigation
of Ralph Capone's income tax
payments.

At the request of Assistant District Attorney William Parrillo,
Commissioner Walker fixed Alter-
ie's bond at $20,000 and continued

Continued on Page 4, Column 1.

To read the full article please go to our website:
www.caponemaygofree.com

time and back in command. So, my Dad argued, there was absolutely no point in Capone trying to fix the jury.

But Dad sensed immediately that trouble was brewing with the judge's selection of the new jury. And was he ever right, because after a trial that lasted only a week or so, the mighty Al Capone got the unheard sentence of 11 years in a federal penitentiary. Nobody could believe anyone, even somebody as notorious as Al Capone, could get a sentence of 11 years for not filing his income taxes.

Naturally, I wanted to know what really happened as I was growing up, and so I would ask: "Dad, was the jury really fixed in the Capone trial?" His answer was always an unequivocal: "YES, THE JURY WAS FIXED, BUT IT WAS FIXED BY THE UNITED STATES GOVERNMENT. IT WAS NOT FIXED BY AL CAPONE."

Besides, Capone's notoriety was so great that the government had to send him up the river, if only to show the public that they were being tough on Organized Crime.

So Capone was sentenced to 11 years in the Atlanta Penitentiary. And after serving a few years there, he had the "honor" of being among the first group of inmates to be housed at Alcatraz in San Francisco Bay.

Like the other prisoners, he got to lay awake at night on "the Rock" and listen to the foghorns and the street sounds of San Francisco across the bay and shiver in that bone-chilling fog that set in every night. Capone got the worst of the worst treatment, but you have to realize that he was never convicted of a heinous crime as was the case with his fellow inmates on Alcatraz.

The simple reason they sent Capone to Alcatraz is that the government had bought that God forsaken pile of rocks from some friends of President Roosevelt, and they had to put a prominent crime boss like Capone there to justify their purchase.

Al Capone had a very rough time of it there on the Rock, and he remained there until he was felled by the little "gift" he got from Jean Harlow called syphilis of the brain. You doctors would call it paresis, but it was Al Capone's undoing because it leads to a paralysis in which all movement is lost.

Al Capone's mug shot above. Al Capone's lover Jean Harlow below. Al Capone was felled by the little "gift" he got from Jean Harlow called syphilis of the brain

So they let him out on parole, and people who had known him, including my father, said the disease had deteriorated Capone's brain to that of a four-year-old. And, like a four-year-old, he would demand an ice cream cone, and cry if nobody gave him one.

Al Capone quietly celebrated his 48th birthday on January 18, 1947, and he died a week later, on January 25, 1947, in the presence of his immediate family.

The MIAMI HERALD reported that: "As word of the death spread, a procession of automobiles began to arrive at the high-walled home (in Florida) where Capone had lived out his anti-climatic years. More callers than the villa has ever had, even in the lush times when gangsters used it as a holiday retreat, were admitted through the gates. A block-long line of sleek, black limousines was parked outside."

And, as a side note to history, you should know that, like most Italians, Al Capone was buried in Mount Carmel Cemetery. But when Capone died, the Catholic Church refused to allow him to be buried on that consecrated ground. So a few years later the mob donated $25,000 to the Catholic Church because Capone's family wanted him to buried with the family that was already there.

So, for $25,000, the Catholic Church decided that Al Capone's ground was not consecrated. Everything around it was, but not his. Today you will find Al Capone resting in his plot of unconsecrated ground at Mount Carmel Cemetery.

Capone was dead, but his legacy as the King of Crime just grew and grew. He is still the subject of movies and books, and he probably always will be. But my Dad knew a different Al Capone than the public did, one who was mild-mannered, and a true Italian in that he would tear up if you told him a sad story.

But, as my father well knew, Capone had a dark side that enabled him to kill his enemies without remorse and then enjoy a good meal right afterwards. Yes, he was remorseless, but he followed a strict code of "crime ethics" that allowed him to only prey on people in the rackets, not on legitimate citizens.

And then there was the charitable Al Capone who started soup kitchens, and put an end to the "Black Hand Letters" that were being sent within the Italian community. This pernicious practice followed us from the old country, and it was simply a means by which a gang would extort money from a family that had made some money in the new country.

My parents received just such a Black Hand Letter from a gang who threatened to kidnap me and my older brother unless they paid $2,000. You can see a copy of the exact letter here in the book. And you can imagine my parents' reaction.

They are working hard to make it in America, and the black hand of anonymous extortion comes unbidden in the mail. As you will see in the letter, the gang directed my parents to wrap the $2,000 in newspaper and leave it at the front door of a storefront on North Ashland Avenue. Before doing as they were told by the extortionists, my parents took the matter to a higher authority and thus were able to determine who owned the vacant store. The owner gladly consented to have two men with shotguns guard the money around the clock to see who would come for it.

And if that wasn't enough, my parents' protectors put two additional shooters in an apartment across the street that had been occupied by an elderly couple, who were sent on vacation to a local hotel until the matter was resolved.

Those four gunmen stood ready to blast the authors of the Black Hand Letter for more than a week, but nobody ever claimed the money.

Our protectors figured that somebody in our own neighborhood gang wrote that letter, so they assigned "Milwaukee Phil" Alderizzio as bodyguard to me and my brother.

Phil was a young guy who was just getting started in the Rackets at the time, so later, when I'd see him, I would say:"You know, Phil, I thought when we were kids you went out to play with us. I didn't know we were supposed to be killed that day." And we'd both have a good laugh over it.

But I digress when I should be telling you about the fortunes of an Outfit that was trying to function without their trusted leader, Al Capone, who was behind bars for about seven years.

President Roosevelt was busy repealing the very Prohibition that had made bootlegging such a profitable business, and then word came that

Extortion letter envelope.

MR MRS PARRILLD

WE WAS GOINGTO
KIDNAPP YOUR KID
BUT WE FIND IT TO
MUCH TROUBLE So
WE ARE GIVKING YOU
A BETTER WAY IF YOU
WANT To TAKE IT WE
NEED 2000 CASH BY
THE END OF NEXT
WEEK, AND IF WE
DONT GET IT YOU
WILL MISS A WIFE
ORE KID SO SEND
AT ONCE THIS TWO
GRAND NO LATER
THAN SAT. THE 17Th
OVER

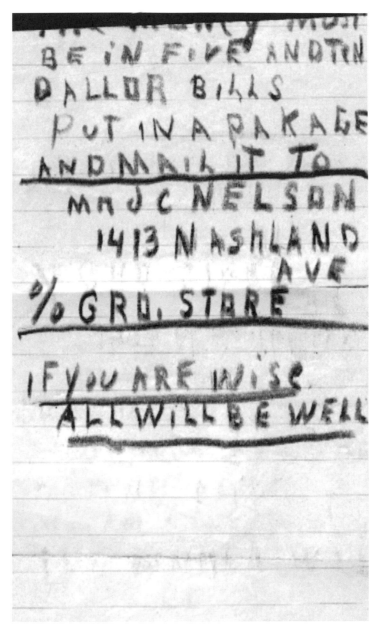

An extortion letter received in 1934 by Donnie's parents. Donnie plans on donating this to the Chicago Historical Society.

Capone was dying from syphilis of brain.

The two questions on everybody's lips were: "Who is the next Al Capone?" and "What will replace bootlegging as a source of revenue?"

They put their heads together and agreed Capone's obvious successor was a new guy named Frank Nitti. All right, his real name was Frank Nitto, but he will forever be known as Frank Nitti. And the newspapers didn't waste any time labeling him "the Enforcer" even though Frank Nitti never carried a gun in his life. Hey, he was a barber by trade who had to lower the chair to reach his customers.

Some people say Frank Nitti was related to Al Capone, but I have yet to see the evidence, and I knew Frank Nitti up until the time he got into trouble. And you will read all about that in the next chapter. But in this chapter you will know that my brother and I loved to play Hearts with Frank Nitti.

We were 10 and 12 at the time, and we thought we were cheating him, but he was wise to us. And at the end of each game, he would give us each a quarter just the same. And that was a lot of money in those days, considering that 15 cents would buy you a milkshake. So my brother and I would bargain with the druggist and get two milkshakes for a quarter.

So there was the whole problem of picking a successor to Capone, and then the Outfit was hit with the winds of "reform" in the form of Chicago's new mayor, Anton Cermak. Yes, the one for whom

Cermak Road is named. That Anton Cermak.

Well, let me tell you that the Outfit had the misfortune to have backed Cermak's opponent, and thus had a vicious new mayor with whom to contend. Cermak hammered the Outfit as soon as he took office, vowing to break it once and for all and replace it with his own "crew."

Cermak launched his offensive by closing up the neighborhood book joints. That hurt because the Outfit had turned to book joints after the repeal of Prohibition turned off the bootlegging spigot.

And to muscle the Outfit, Cermak had his own muscle command the Chicago Police Department, such as a certain captain he posted at the Maxwell Street District on the near South Side.

When the Outfit went to Cermak's captain so they could continue their booking, he demanded an exorbitant kick-back that would have put the ka-bosh on the whole racket. So, being astute businessmen, the Outfit guys told the new captain that they were going to pay him the same "consideration" as they had paid his predecessor, $1,500 a month. Cermak's captain says: "No, it's not enough. I'll put my own man in to run all the book joints in MY district."

To which the Outfit responds: "You play it our way, or nobody but nobody makes book in this district."

So the captain installs a man named McDonald as a bookie. He's going to play it Cermak's way, no matter what those wiseguys say. And guess what happens: this McDonald character, who has the full faith and trust of the Cermak administration behind him, walks out of his book joint on the second day of operation and gets popped by an unknown assailant. He got Taylor Street Justice.

The new captain stews on this for about two weeks and then decides to take the same $1,500 that his predecessor was getting.

All's fair in love and war, right?

But Mayor Anton Cermak is not taking this lying down. So he sends two coppers to take out Frank Nitti, and all they succeed in doing is plugging him in the back and leaving him for dead. But Frank Nitti is one tough customer, and he lives, and there is hell to pay. And I mean Anton Cermak's life itself.

I know all about the legend that Mayor Cermak took a bullet for President Roosevelt down there in Florida, and died a hero.

But let me tell it to you straight: The Outfit found a guy in New England who was almost dead of cancer and told him they'd give his widow $25,000 after he killed Cermak. The poor man wants to take care of his wife, so he shoots the Mayor of Chicago, not the President of the United States, while they are watching this parade in Miami. And he conveniently dies of cancer before they can bring him to trial. Taylor Street Justice was served again.

Cermak's cronies have to save face, so they concoct the now famous story that the assassin was really after President Roosevelt, and that Cermak

The question on everybody's lips was: "Who is the next Al Capone?

*Frank Nitti succeeded Capone when
Capone was sentenced to jail in 1931.*

took the bullet for his president.

So: Anton Cermak 0; Frank Nitti 1.

Game over, and Frank Nitti continued to run the Chicago Outfit until 1942 when he was one of eight people indicted for shaking down the movie unions in Hollywood.

But never mind that, because the Frank Nitti I knew was a gentle man who gave me and my brother a quarter even after we cheated at Hearts. I just cannot picture Frank Nitti as a hardened criminal running the rackets. That was not the Frank Nitti I knew when I was growing up on Taylor Street.

Before Frank Nitti went to trial, he went to a railroad yard, and according to two engineers on a train idling nearby in the freight yard, Frank took out his gun and fired one round through his hat. He shot the second round into his head and died instantly.

It was 1942, and Frank Nitti left the Outfit in the best shape ever, with gambling revenues more than making up for the loss of the bootlegging.

But Frank Nitti left the Outfit by his own hand, and they were again faced with that terrible dilemma of choosing a new leader.

Would the Outfit survive?

You will have to keep reading to find out, but I can assure you that you won't be disappointed.

And now, before you turn off your reading lamp, I wanted to share this touching little story of how my Irish wife and I were watching television one night when the news came on, and they said a body had just been found in a car in a parking lot

*Paul Ricca succeeded Frank Nitti in 1942
after Nitti committed suicide.*

*Paul Ricca appointed Tony Accardo (above) to be "The Boss"
after he was convicted on the movie extortion trial and went to jail in
1943. Accardo's nickname was 'Joe B." The B stood for Batters.*

In 1950, as the government was putting too much pressure on Joe B.
Joe B. then made Sam Giancana "The Boss."

at O'Hare Field.

My Irish wife turns to me and says: "I bet that's an Italian." And I say: "Well, you'll see. It may not be."

But sure enough, the victim turned out to have some typical Italian name like "Angelo" or "Bagagaloopo." And, sure enough, they had found two bullet holes in his head, and he had of course been stuffed in the trunk of his own car.

So my smart-aleck Irish wife says: "Don't any of you dagos ever die a natural death?"

To which I can only reply: "That IS a natural death for a dago."

Donnie Parrillo

CHAPTER FOUR

THE OUTFIT
(Birth of a Monster)

The Chicago crime syndicate was a model of business success until 1933 when President Roosevelt took away their bootlegging bounty by repealing the Prohibition Act.

What was an enterprising Outfit to do?

Why turn to bookmaking, gambling and controlling the local labor unions, that's what. And with labor unions on the rise, it was only natural that the crime bosses should look to them for a little "financial support." If you know what I mean.

And gambling looked a lot more lucrative to most of those men than the booze business that had come with a heavy price tag in the form of overzealous G Men.

So let's look at Chicago in 1933. Most of your bookmakers were Jewish, but they were not backed by an army or gang. That was a plus for the

Italian-dominated Outfit, because it meant they could demand their piece of the action from those independent bookmakers without fear of retaliation from a Jewish outfit. And by demand, I mean the old "your money or your life."

So your independent Jewish bookmaker in Chicago had two choices: play along with the Italians and give them their percentage in return for their protection, or leave town.

Well, there was a third option: end up with bullets in your head and your body stuffed in a car trunk.

But there were a few bookmakers who thought they could defy the Outfit because they had the backing of their local gangs. But they didn't stay protected for too long, because the Outfit always got what it wanted in those days, and what they wanted in those days was total control of the bookmaking business in Chicago.

I tell you, business classes could learn from their methods.

Anyway, the Outfit quickly filled their depleted coffers with their take from the bookmaking operations around Chicagoland, and they then set their sites on an even more promising prospect: the labor unions.

But this was not going to be any walk in the park because most of the unions were controlled by some very tough Irishmen. And those "micks" were not about to step aside and let a bunch of "dagos" take over.

And they weren't the only ones standing in the

way of the Outfit's total control of the Chicago rackets. You had people on the West Side like "Klondike" O'Donnell, "Three-Finger" White, and Barney Grogan who were not about to yield to the Outfit.

Nor was "Pollock" Joe Saltis going to give up the near South Side, and this aforementioned McErlane was not going to roll over and play dead a bit farther south.

Spike O'Donnell had the far South Side sewn up for himself, and the Outfit knew that the tough customer named Frank LaPorte was running the show south of the city in Chicago Heights, where, as I have said, most of the people were Italian.

Looking north, the Outfit saw a lucrative territory dominated by the unlikable likes of Dion O'Bannon and Bugs Moran and their respective gangs of thugs, like the dreaded Gusenburg Brothers who provided Moran's muscle. O'Bannon had everything from the river up to Diversey Avenue, and Moran controlled the turf from there to Evanston.

Moran's gang, of course, made world history by being wiped out on St. Valentine's Day, 1929 in that garage on North Clark Street, and Moran later died in prison while doing time for a bank he had robbed.

So the Chicago area was really a big chessboard for the Outfit to take over, and, like chess masters, they planned three moves ahead and mercilessly took over each new territory with nothing but "checkmate" in mind. And by territory, I mean the boundaries of the various districts of the Chicago Police Department.

Their Roman ancestors would take over a territory and install a "governor," and so the successors of Julius Caesar would install two of their own "made men" as "owners" of the turf that they had just claimed for themselves.

The two owners employed a "crew" of four trusted compatriots who would go forth and muscle those who didn't care to cooperate with the new order of business.

When one of the two "owners" in a district died, the top man in the crew would succeed him as a "made man."

Cicero was so lucrative that the Outfit had three made men, or owners, running the show there, and they put four made men in charge of the biggest prize of all: downtown Chicago.

The "Loop" wasn't only the biggest crime package in all of Chicagoland, it was number one in the nation for less-than-legal business opportunities.

And, by the way, the entire downtown district was in the First Ward of Chicago that I would later serve as alderman.

And to further establish control of their territories, the Outfit used their growing political clout to engineer the assignment of their own police captain to each district. The crime boss's captain, in turn, would request the transfer of trusted sergeants, lieutenants, and patrolmen to his command.

So you had muscle both in uniform and in plain

clothes. But you also had your legendary independent operators like 43rd Ward Alderman Mathias "Paddy" Bauler who somehow kept his head above those troubled waters.

Famous for his quote, "Chicago ain't ready for reform," Paddy Bauler served with me in the City Council, and he told me a story of the St. Valentine's Day Massacre that bears repeating right here and now:

Moments after the massacre, "Machine Gun" Jack McGurn rushes into Paddy Bauler's tavern on the North Side with two police uniforms that were used to disguise the gunmen who had mowed down Moran's gang.

Pointing to the potbelly stove burning brightly in the middle of the tavern, McGurn thrusts the uniforms into Alderman Bauler's hands and says: "Here, burn these right away. But take the buttons off first, because those brass buttons might not burn that easy."

Paddy Bauler does as he is told, and he goes on to become a very wealthy man from both Prohibition and bookmaking.

Alderman Charlie Webber was another legendary independent operator, and he controlled a territory just north of Paddy Bauler's freewheeling 43rd Ward. Webber made the mistake of not turning his car's motor off one night, and, because he and his wife slept over the garage, they failed to wake up the next morning.

But the Outfit did wake up to a brave new world in 1938 when they realized they had "eliminated" all serious competition. They were in charge of all the rackets and any nefarious endeavors that would bring in money. They had declared "checkmate" and won the chess game for control of the true crime center of America: Chicago.

Chicago was theirs, but an undreamed prize loomed before them: the Irish-controlled Northwest suburbs. And they gladly rushed in to fill the power vacuum left when Roger Touhy went to jail for kidnapping John "Jake the Barber" Factor, and "Terrible Tommie" Touhy moved to Arizona.

A side note to crime history you should know: after Roger Touhy and five other inmates were caught after escaping from Stateville in 1942, the FBI got involved in their case, because the feds said they had failed to provide their local draft boards with forwarding addresses.

How thoughtful of the FBI.

So with Touhy and the rest out of the way, the Outfit ruled over all of Chicagoland, and they fueled their crime engine with truckloads of money that bookmaking brought in. It was time to move on the last lucrative prize, control of the labor unions and their piles of money. They took control of the unions in the usual manner, they muscled their men onto the payrolls, and they could thus show the government that they were earning legitimate income.

Now the Outfit could shake down four-square businessmen by either calling a strike or taking payoffs for averting a strike.

Win-win either way.

The Outfit looted the treasuries of the local unions to fund their own operations, and so what if some people went to jail?

The Outfit continued building their crime empire, and they were the most powerful entity in the City of Chicago by 1940.

And that brings us to the question: is it wrong to gamble?

Gambling is undoubtedly the most fascinating entertainment ever devised by man, so let's look at the good and bad of gambling, starting with the "pristine" National Football League, or NFL.

When the NFL started, most of the owners had affiliations with a crime syndicate in one part of the country or another. Take the 2009 Super Bowl Champions, the Pittsburgh Steelers, as an example. Steelers owner Art Rooney was often seen at the racetrack or bookmaker placing bets. Not only that, but Rooney was sanctioned by the local crime syndicate to be the only bookmaker at Pittsburgh racetracks. But why would a person bet with a bookmaker at the track instead of at the window?

Two reasons:

1. If they won a lot of money, they got paid in cash and did not have to pay income tax on it.

2. If they made a huge wager and placed it in the window at the track, the odds on their horse decreased rapidly.

Art Rooney ran book for most of his life, and although it was his only source of income, it made him rich enough to buy the Pittsburgh Steelers.

I have some more dirty laundry from the so-called pristine NFL that I would like to share with you: the old Chicago Cardinals who played in Comiskey Park on the South Side. The Bears, of course, were a bigger draw, so they played on the North Side in Wrigley Field. A West Side book-maker named Charles Bidwell owned the Cardinals. Bidwell also owned Sportsman Park Racetrack in Cicero with several partners, some of whom were members of the Chicago Outfit.

Shocking, isn't it?

The Chicago Cardinals left town long ago and are now known as the Arizona Cardinals. And, yes, they are the team that lost the 2009 Super Bowl to the Pittsburgh Steelers. The Cardinals left Chicago, but they are still owned by the Bidwell family and operated by Charles Bidwell's grandsons.

Three other NFL teams were owned by men with dubious reputations: - the Los Angeles Rams, the San Diego Chargers, and the New Orleans Saints.

Big bets were won when these teams played one another, because the coaches were "ordered" to "fix" not the outcome but the "spread" on the "over/under."

Keep the ball on the ground, they were told, and nobody gets hurt. Keeping the ball on the ground, not in the air, almost always ensured that the final score would favor whoever had bet on the "under."

This grounding of games wasn't completely foolproof, but they got five favorable outcomes out of the six games they fixed. And if I have to explain who "they" were, then I'll know you haven't been paying close enough attention.

This caper came to an untimely end when the players got suspicious and started asking their coaches questions like: "How come last week we passed 45 times, and this week we only passed 15 times?"

And call it a coincidence or just being in the wrong place at the wrong time, but the owner of the Los Angeles Rams drowned in two feet of water in the Pacific Ocean shortly after this little scheme was hatched.

And here's a dirty little NFL story that really hits close to home: An NFL rule states that no injury to a player can be made public after practice on Friday afternoon, usually 5 p.m.

But the Bears' legendary running back, Gayle Sayers, stepped in a hole during a warm-up on Saturday before the big game on Sunday against the Cleveland Browns at Wrigley Field.

Well, they took Sayers to the hospital where the doctor x-rayed him and said: "He's not going to play tomorrow. He's not going to play for a few weeks."

This is huge, because the Bears were six-point favorites over the Browns. So, instead of acting like a bunch of good little Boy Scouts, the Bears hierarchy called their favorite bookies around the city and bet on Cleveland.

That's right, the Bears brass bet on the Browns, because they knew their star player was on the DL.

And without Sayers, the Bears could not stop the Browns, so those Bears insiders called people who had lines of credit in Las Vegas to put money on Cleveland before it was to be announced that Sayers had been sidelined by the injury he had sustained on Saturday.

Now, those Las Vegas bookies were no dummies, so they smelled a rat when they saw thousands upon thousands of dollars come pouring down on the Cleveland Browns.

The Vegas gambling houses, in turn, suspended all bets on the Bears-Browns game for two hours. When they reopened the betting lines, they made Cleveland the six-point favorite, and the Browns obliged by not only winning the game, but by beating the spread.

The NFL officially frowns on gambling, but they know that their TV ratings would evaporate without gambling. And if you didn't have "money on the game" would you read all about it in your local newspapers? No, and the NFL franchises wouldn't be worth anywhere near what they are valued at today without more than a few friendly bets on each and every game.

Still skeptical that gambling runs football? Then try this little experiment, which I have successfully conducted three times: go to a Super Bowl party and see how many people are actually watching the game. You will, as I did on three separate occasions, see people eating, drinking, laughing, and socializing. You won't see a single set of eyes glued to the game. But when it comes down to the last play of each quarter, there will be a deafening silence as everyone wants to see if he or she won the pool. Those who did will scream with joy, and the losers will cry like little babies. But not over the game and the two teams. No, it's all in the bet!

My contention is that without betting, legal or illegal - and much more if it is bet illegally, there wouldn't be any National Football League.

No bets, no NFL.

It's that simple, and so is the answer to my question: "Is gambling bad?"

Gambling, as my Roman ancestors discovered while betting on the chariot races, is a source of great entertainment.

Gambling generates cash and drives our economy.

But there is one time when gambling IS bad, and that IS when you lose!

Donnie Parrillo

CHAPTER FIVE

SAM GIANCANA
(A NEW BOSS, "THE CIGAR")

When Sam Giancana was a wild young man in the old Italian neighborhood, they called him "Mooney" because he was just plain squirrelly. He was nuts, and no one could predict what he would do next. So he was called Mooney like a horse that looks at the full moon too long.

When Sam Giancana was inducted into that hall of infamy known as the Outfit and became a "made man," they simply called him "Mo."

And when he became the Boss of the Chicago Outfit, they called him "the Cigar," because he liked cigars. Kind of obvious, isn't it?

Anyway, the young Sam Giancana, the kid they called Mooney, was always in trouble with the law.

How bad was Mooney? Well, people used to say: "He was one tough guy without an army behind him." An army of one, as we might say today.

If Sam Giancana had been born with that silver spoon in his mouth and sent to the best college and given all the connections the rich in this country have, on careers day he still would have said he wanted to be in the rackets.

That was just the way he was, and Mooney's modus operandi, or m.o., was to rob the occasional jewelry store, and then maybe crack a safe in a State Street store or two. And he wasn't above hitting banks.

But to show how nuts he really was when he was young, I have to tell you that Mooney didn't hesitate to rob some of the Outfit's own book joints.

Talk about brass balls, because if they had caught him, and this was before he was initiated as a made man, he would have been killed instantly and his body dumped in the Chicago River as an example of "Taylor Street Justice."

When Sam was only 20 he was tried for murder, but the eyewitness for the state was murdered before he could testify. And so the young Sam Giancana was acquitted.

So how did this wild child known as Mooney became a made man in the Chicago Outfit? Sam had two paths: one, he could kill his way into the organization, or he could simply show the Outfit how to make tons of money.

Sam easily completed the first requirement before his first razor got rusty, and he had it in that fine Italian head of his a foolproof money making scheme for both the Outfit and, of course, himself.

Sam Giancana

Sam Giancana was going to become a made man all the way, and he began his quest in the early 1940s when he met the infamous "Jones Brothers" while serving a jail sentence for one of his many indiscretions.

This pair of black gangsters bragged to anyone who would listen about how many millions of dollars they were making in what was then called the "Numbers Racket" on their native South Side of Chicago.

Young Sam Giancana was all ears, because the New York City Numbers Racket was nationally famous for helping the average housewife make ends meet.

What I mean is Mrs. Working Class would go buy what she needed at the local store and then tell the clerk to "buy a lottery ticket for me" with the change.

For reasons that only a sociologist could explain, the Numbers Racket was more popular with blacks than whites. In fact, it was part of the fabric of black life not only in New York but here in Chicago where those clever criminals, the Jones Brothers, were operating.

The stores in the black neighborhoods maintained Policy Wheels and sold the tickets, and the Jones Brothers, and that's Brother with a capital B because they were a true operation, would send their runners to collect the money.

So Sam Giancana absorbed all this knowledge of the profitable Numbers Racket while he was cooling his heels in jail, and he went straight to the

Outfit upon his release and told them about the Numbers Racket. Well, they did balk at first, because they didn't think they could take over a black territory. Just couldn't be done, they said.

But then the Jones Brothers got out of jail, and some anonymous person had a little chat with them, and they immediately decided it was in their best interests to move to sunny Mexico. Adios Jones Brothers and hello Outfit who gladly took over their half of the South Side Numbers Racket. Their only obstacle to total control was a smooth operator named Theodore Roe.

He would have to be dealt with, but first the Outfit consolidated their new holdings by installing the Manno Brothers in a front operation that was a Chrysler-Plymouth dealership in front, and a bookmaking operation in back complete with the requisite big table.

You have to hand it to the Outfit when it comes to making good on an even better business plan.

Reliable sources tell me that runners would appear throughout the day and dump sacks of cash on that big table. Then their good Italian wives would count the cash, most of which was just pocket change from working stiffs.

Sam Giancana had turned the Outfit onto a truly big score that was so lucrative that they gave the Manno Brothers $250,000 a month for their troubles, and, of course, kept the rest for themselves.

Yes, we're talking a cool $6 million in annual profits for the Outfit just from their exciting new

Numbers Racket. The papers and the government said the Outfit was taking in $80K a day, but you should know by now not to trust what the media and government tell you.

But you should know that the Outfit was into some serious money when they filled that void down there on the South Side left by the Jones Brothers. And one of the great things about the Numbers Racket is that collecting on bets that ranged from 50 cents to three dollars was easy.

It was all face-to-face with people you knew from your neighborhood, and so the bookies didn't have to bury the gamblers, and thus the Outfit didn't have to extort money from them. It was, as we say now, a win-win operation.

Meanwhile, our man Giancana is rising to the top of the Chicago Outfit, and when he had taken total control in 1952, he reckoned it was time to see if that aforementioned operator, Theodore Roe, might not like to part with his half of the Numbers Racket. So, following their classic business model, the Outfit sent "The Cigar" Giancana, "Teets" Bataglia, and "Fat Lenny" Caifano, to make Theodore Roe a reasonable offer for his half of the racket. All three were made men and professional killers. But Roe wasn't about to roll over and play dead because he had built up an army of his own with his enormous profits.

So when Roe and the "business associate" he was riding with saw three white guys from Chicago pull up beside them in another car, they opened fire without hesitation and killed "Fat Lenny" Caifano.

Teets and the Cigar dodged the bullets and escaped on foot, and having heard Sam Giancana tell the story, I can tell you that they ran all through that black neighborhood desperately looking for a way out.

The Cigar told me that after he and Teets had gotten separated, he flagged down a taxicab and took the cab back to safe territory. Teets never told me how he got out, but he obviously had the street smarts to live to tell about it.

And the newspapers, as usual, told the wrong story, saying that Theodore Roe killed Fat Lenny and shot at The Cigar and Teets. But the actual shooter was that "business associate" I mentioned earlier, and, surprise, surprise, he was a police captain, whose name I choose to withhold.

This was suicide for anybody to kill one of their made men, and they evened the score immediately.

The Outfit unleashed their "vendetta" on August 4, 1952 as Theodore Roe was calmly leaving his flat to get into his car. Suddenly there was more lead than air, and Roe's blind wife, who was up in their apartment, later told police that she knew her husband was a goner as soon as she heard all those shots.

Theodore Roe's untimely end put the Outfit in total control of the South Side Numbers Racket. And when they saw that blacks were moving to the West Side, they wisely "cornered" the Numbers Racket there as well.

You would think no one would be crazy enough to challenge the Outfit's total control of the

Numbers Racket, but in 1963 a certain Ben Lewis got himself elected Alderman of the 24th Ward and declared himself boss of all the rackets in his ward. Guess what? Lewis had only been in office for a month when they found him handcuffed in his office with his head ventilated by lead. So ended Ben Lewis and his foolish quest and so added another ward to the Outfit's profitable empire.

And by profitable, I mean that the income from the Numbers Racket was enormous. They made almost as much from the Numbers as they were getting out of their illegal book joints and crap games.

So the Outfit took the handling of the Numbers Racket away from the Manno Brothers and had their own people count and stash the cash. And just so you know, all four Manno Brothers were later indicted and convicted of income tax evasion.

It always bewilders me how somebody who reports an income of $15,000 or $20,000 a year suddenly ends up buying a $1 million home. Obviously crime and money corrupt, and criminals can't change their high-rolling ways.

The Numbers Racket died from complications due to competition from state lotteries, off-track betting, and casinos in the early 1970s.

The newspapers celebrated its passing, saying it had been a "tax on poor people" and what a "terrible, vicious racket" it had been.

Hogwash!

You want to talk about a tax on poor people

that doesn't benefit those same poor people, consider the Illinois Lottery that was hailed by the media for funneling 100 percent of its income into children's education.

Dream on, because last year in Illinois, only about 13 percent of Lottery proceeds went to education, with remaining 87 percent going into that open cookie jar known as the General Fund.

And whose hands do you find in the cookie jar? If I have to spell "politician" out for you, you really were born yesterday.

The Numbers Racket was a diversion for poor people, and it put money in many an empty pocket, but like all rackets, it had a very limited life. When the Outfit controlled all the illegal book joints in Cook County, everybody, including the media, would tell the people how bad it was, how ruthless the operators were, and how immoral gambling was.

Fair enough, but then how was the State of Illinois any holier than the Outfit by allowing gambling casinos to corner that market?

If gambling is so evil, why do we have off-track betting parlors in residential areas, and gambling boats on the rivers and lake?

The Numbers Racket simply could not compete with the onslaught of "legal" lotteries, casinos, and betting parlors that were praised for putting their profits in the hands of our benevolent government and for not preying on those unsuspecting poor people.

Never mind that almost all of the money now

goes into the General Fund instead of into the classrooms where it is needed. A small detail that you won't hear much about on the news.

But I digress when I should be charting the rise to power of Sam "the Cigar" Giancana who was crowned a "made man" in 1944 after he had helped the Outfit to consolidate all of the rackets in Chicago.

Giancana continued his ascent by becoming the Boss of Organized Crime about 1950. He was literally taking the hot seat, because the FBI was recording their every sneeze by then, but Sam had an ego second to none, and was quite content to be the boss of bosses. But he was wise to the ways of the FBI, meaning that you could be sitting with him at a Cubs game at Wrigley Field, and he would talk in whispers. Somebody could have been listening, and somebody probably was. So Sam Giancana would never say anything out loud, no matter where he was.

And I speak with authority, because I knew the man most of my life. He would come to our neighborhood to consult with our local boss who was a made man, and my father, and the boss would tell Sam, "take the kids to school and come right back."

How many kids do you know who had Sam Giancana take them to school in the morning?

Well now you know one, and you should know that when I was young I called him "Mr. Sam."

When I got older I addressed him as "Sam," never "Mooney, Mo, or the Cigar."

Sam Giancana and Phyllis McGuire (right.)

The Sam Giancana I knew was a congenial man with a rough-talking way about him. He didn't swear so much as just have a poor command of the English language.

And his fatal flaw, certainly for a career member of the Underworld, was a love of the limelight and a craving for headlines. The normal wise guy would walk into a restaurant and head for the back corner and hide behind his menu, but not Sam. No, he would make a grand entrance so that everyone and his brother knew that "the Cigar" had arrived.

And with his love of the limelight, Sam naturally gravitated to the glitter of Hollywood where he dated starlets and hung out with producers. And so the love of his life became Phyllis McGuire who performed with her sisters in Las Vegas.

Phyllis McGuire was a minister's daughter, but that didn't stop her from falling for a crime boss from Chicago. She and Sam had quite an affair going until he had to go to Mexico.

Mexico?

Yes, Sam went to Mexico because the feds were breathing down his neck, and he had certainly aided their investigations with that love of the limelight of his.

Plus, the other guys in the Outfit were tiring of his flashy ways and demanding that he live the same low-profile lives that they did. Who did he think he was, anyway?

Sam had his affair with Phyllis McGuire for all the world to see, and he publicly associated with the likes of Frank Sinatra, Dean Martin, Sammy Davis Junior, Joey Bishop, Peter Lawford, and Marilyn Monroe. Nice company if you can afford it, and Sam certainly could.

And if that wasn't enough, Sam presented himself as a doctor, and went under the name of "Dr. Mooney" when he stayed at Sinatra's house in Palm Springs.

I know many people who met him at Frank Sinatra's house and had no idea who he was. But the Actors' Union certainly knew the real Sam Giancana.

The Outfit controlled the union, and Sam controlled the Outfit so he got to control who got certain roles in certain movies.

Take Yul Brynner for example. Sam decreed that Yul Brynner was perfect for the lead in "The

King and I," and a grateful Brynner sent him a Yorkshire terrier.

Remember Frank Sinatra in that World War II classic, "From Here to Eternity?" Ever wonder how a guy who was more famous for singing than acting got the part of Maggio in the movie?

Well, Sam and company told the producer that he either put Sinatra in a leading role, or he simply would have no movie. The producer squawked that Sinatra was too cocky and unreliable, but Sam and company assured him that Frank would suddenly become the most disciplined actor he had ever worked with, and, wonder of wonders, he was.

But there is a law of physics that says that what goes up must come down, and Sam Giancana's fortunes were in free-fall by 1965 when the government "invited" him to testify under immunity before the Grand Jury in Chicago.

Come and sing like a canary, Uncle Sam said to Sam Giancana.

Sam refused and so served a year in the Cook County Jail. He had planned to go to Mexico the day he got out of jail. His associates in the Outfit were delighted, because it meant they could go about their business under the radar of the press and the feds.

Everyone was happy, especially Sam who stayed in sunny Mexico for nine long years. He probably would have stayed much longer, but then the Mexican government, for reasons that are still unclear, suddenly declared him persona non grata.

They were so eager to have him out of their hair

that they flew him back in the middle of the night to Chicago where he was greeted by newspaper photographers who captured him getting off the plane still in his pajamas and badly in need of a shave.

And if that wasn't enough humiliation for one crime boss, Sam had only been back in town a few weeks when he got a subpoena from the Senate Racketeering Committee. It seemed they had a few questions about certain "questionable" activities of his.

Only Sam Giancana can say for sure what was in the mind of Sam Giancana at that critical point. Some were sure he was going to ask for immunity and then rat out the entire Outfit. Others said he would keep his mouth shut and then muscle his way back to the top again. But only Sam knew for sure what Sam was thinking, and he wasn't saying.

But he was certainly doing something he loved to do on that summer night in 1976 when he was making sausage in his basement for a friend.

It was a most Italian thing to be doing, and Sam Giancana was Italian through and through. And he died that night of "natural Italian causes" when someone who was obviously known to him emptied the contents of a .22-caliber gun into his neck.

The Cigar was extinguished.

Sam Giancana was dead, and an era was at an end.

Want to know who did it? All will be revealed shortly, but I will tell you right here that the FBI initially disagreed with me. But when they finally came out with their report, they agreed that I had been right all along and that they had the wrong information.

You will never meet a more colorful guy than Sam. He came from nowhere and rose to become one of the most powerful people in the United States. That is why I put his picture on the cover of my book, there between Al Capone and John F. Kennedy.

Sam Giancana ruled the Outfit for 14 years, which is a long time to be the boss of that organization and keep your head about you.

I will never forget Sam Giancana. Never.

Sam Giancana Headlines - for more information please go to our website: www.caponemaygofree.com

Super Slam winners

Turn to
Page 5

RAIN?

CHICAGO
Sun-Times

TURF FINAL
The City and Suburbs

Saturday, June 21, 1975

Hit man's target

Mob silenced Giancana

See Pages 3, 6

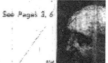

How killer got in?

Eye mob hit man in Giancana murder

CHAPTER SIX

"THE CIGAR WANTS TO SEE YOU"
(A TOUGH OFFER TO REFUSE)

My heart raced when an old-time bookmaker appeared at my desk at my newly acquired National Bank and gave me that simple message:

"THE CIGAR WANTS TO SEE YOU."

My heart was pounding just to think that Sam "the Cigar" Giancana wanted to see me. Why? I was as paralyzed with curiosity as I was with fear. Why would the Cigar want to see me, a freshly minted bank president?

But, coming from the old neighborhood, I had learned not to ask why, but to simply acknowledge the Cigar's messenger. I knew to take him seriously because he had been around the track a few times as both a bookmaker and as a politician from Chinatown. He was "on top" of the "underworld," and he was right from Central Casting with his big "pinkie" ring and his even bigger cigar.

I knew him to see him, and I knew that he had come to see me on behalf of the most powerful crime boss in the country.

"THE CIGAR WANTS TO SEE YOU."

There it was: Sam Giancana, the uncontested ruler of the Chicago Outfit, wanted to see me. This was the Cigar who ruled a consolidated crime empire in Chicago with unbelievable reach and power.

Hoping that the messenger wouldn't hear my heart pounding in my chest, I heard him out as calmly as I could and thus learned that the Cigar's instructions were as follows: "Tomorrow afternoon at 2 o'clock, go and visit your father's grave."

Of course. I was to go and visit my father's grave at Mount Carmel Cemetery, about 10 miles west of Chicago. Most Italians are buried there, including Al Capone himself. (But you already know that from reading chapter 3.)

I never needed an excuse to visit my father's grave, but I was curious. So I wanted to say to the Cigar's messenger: "Why my father's grave?"

But, being from the old neighborhood, I had learned to keep my mouth shut, and I kept it shut then and there.

I sent the messenger on his way with my consent to visit my father's grave the next day, and that night I took my wife out for what I was seriously thinking might be my own "Last Supper."

You don't get a summons to see Sam Giancana at your father's grave and think everything is going to be hunky-dory. So my "Lace Curtain" Irish wife sees the worry on my Italian brow and wants to know what's up, but I couldn't tell her.

She was Irish and from the better side of the tracks, and she just didn't know the ways of my old neighborhood. So I just sat there feeling worried and miserable and picking at my food.

Why me?

Why did the Cigar want to see me?

I tossed and turned all night, and, the first thing the next morning, I told my secretary that I would be away from the bank all day. No details. Nothing. Just that I would be gone for the day.

But what a beautiful day in late October it was! October days in Chicago are to die for, and if I was going to die that day, well, then at least the Cigar had picked a real beauty for me.

So with at least a beautiful October day to comfort me, I left my place in downtown Chicago at 1 o'clock that afternoon and drove to Mount Carmel Cemetery with my mind racing.

For starters, I knew I didn't have to go because I didn't owe the Cigar anything. I was not on his pad or his payroll. The only thing I ever felt that I might owe him was a second-generation friendship.

Sam Giancana, you see, would often drop in on my father in the morning when my brother and I were very young.

Dad was Giancana's lawyer, so they had business to discuss, and then the Cigar would drive my brother and me to school. So, out of sheer respect for those good, old days, I was driving out to the cemetery to meet him.

But I couldn't keep from worrying throughout that 45-minute drive to destiny about just what the big "Magaffer" might want from me. What was he going to ask me to do? I hoped it wouldn't be something illegal, and I was pretty sure it wouldn't, but I was on my way to see the Boss of Bosses, and anything was possible.

I had last seen Sam Giancana at one of his favorite haunts, the Armory Lounge in Forest Park. The food was excellent, prepared by an old man and his wife, and it was an intimate setting with seating for 40 or 50.

The Cigar ate more meals at the Armory Lounge than any other restaurant, and so it was no surprise that both the CIA and the FBI bugged the area where Giancana usually sat. And that caused a serious clash between those two agencies in Washington, because organized crime was the province of the FBI, not the CIA.

So why, the FBI wanted to know, did the CIA bug the boss of the Chicago Outfit?

Simple: the nation's spies were bugging Giancana so they could blackmail him into killing Fidel Castro for them. The CIA actually promised the Cigar immunity for doing it, even though they didn't have the authority to make such a promise.

The CIA sweetened the deal by promising Giancana all the legal gambling in Cuba if he made Castro disappear. But Giancana assured the CIA that he had already won such assurances from the Kennedys.

I personally think Giancana was ready to take out Castro, but I don't think the rest of his people were up for such a high-risk game. Plus, Sam was wise to the ways of Joe Kennedy and his clan, so he told the CIA that JFK would take care of Castro, sooner or later.

Need I mention the disastrous "Bay of Pigs" episode of 1961? The Bay of Pigs invasion was such a total disaster, in my view, that it led directly to the assassination of President John F. Kennedy on November 22, 1963.

Some connected people were seriously angry with Kennedy because it was their friends, partners, and relatives who were mowed down on that beach in Cuba by Castro and his army who had been tipped off that they were coming. And coming, I should add, without proper air and naval support.

You ask me, it was all a set-up. And, if you ask me, I'll tell you that Kennedy simply didn't want Organized Crime to regain control of the multi-million dollar gambling operations on an island only 90 miles from the United States. Kennedy simply didn't want them to have that much power.

And now back to the longest 45 minutes of my life as I drove out to Mount Carmel Cemetery for my meeting with the Cigar. I thought of that last time I had seen him at the Armory Lounge there in Forest Park just west of Chicago. It was January of 1961 and I was there with some friends to plan our annual golf trip to sunnier climes.

We concluded our business, and I was leaving the restaurant when a familiar voice called to me:

"Donnie, come on over and have a drink with me."

It was the man who used to drive me and my brother to school in the morning, so I gladly sat down with the Cigar.

Having an ego second to none, he immediately started in with: "You never thought you'd see the day that I'd elect a guy President of the United States, would you?"

He was referring, of course, to John F. Kennedy's narrow victory in November 1960 when the First Ward of Chicago put him in the White House instead of Richard Nixon.

I listened politely, because I knew that he had a hair trigger on his temper. And I politely and delicately put it to Sam Giancana that "young kids" like Jack Kennedy had been born with silver spoons in their mouths and thus had no appreciation for anything anybody did for them.

In Kennedy's opinion, I said, the world owed it all to him and people like him. I've said I had seen that happen time and again, and I told Sam that the rich are the poorest tippers, if they even tip at all.

I also reminded the Cigar of his appearance with Frank Costello before the Senate Rackets Committee compliments of the President's little brother, Bobby Kennedy.

Frank Costello, as you may recall, was Ambassador Joe Kennedy's partner in bootlegging, but that didn't stop Bobby Kennedy from trying to belittle him and Sam Giancana in front of the whole country.

The Cigar shrugged it off, saying it was just the

Kennedys' way of telling the public they were really fighting Organized Crime from the top down. "But we already had them in our pocket," the Cigar told me. "The deal was already made, and we were pretty sure with all the power and money we had going for us, we were going to be able to elect this Jack Kennedy guy President of the United States."

Because I had never met any of the colorful Kennedys, Sam gladly described them for me, starting with JFK, whom he liked. He said John F. Kennedy was a funny guy who loved nothing better than chasing skirts. Bobby, he said, was just the opposite. More reserved than his older brother and harder to get along with. But, like big brother Jack, Bobby was forever chasing women, and Sam gladly told me about all the "broads" he had fixed the Kennedy brothers up with.

And so, with the Kennedys in control of the White House, Sam said he was ready to reap his harvest and become one of the most powerful men in not only the United States, but in the world.

The Cigar then told me how he thought things were going to shake out, but I was too shaken as I neared the cemetery to focus on his predictions.

So more about Sam Giancana and the Kennedys a bit later in this book, and now on to my dreaded meeting with him at my father's grave.

I knew Sam Giancana was a fair man who was always good for his word, so I clung to that comforting thought as I entered the vast cemetery and approached my father's grave.

I nervously looked about for other cars and saw

only one old pick-up truck with some shovels and brooms in back that a cemetery caretaker might use. And sure enough, there was just such a caretaker planting flowers on a grave just a few from my father's. He looked perfectly normal and non-threatening, so I didn't give him another thought as I got out of my car.

I walked to my father's grave, looked at my watch and saw that it was 10 minutes to 2, and started praying for my father's eternal rest. I was in the middle of my prayer when I heard a familiar voice call, "Donnie? Donnie, are you alone?"

I looked up, and there was the man I had mistaken for the cemetery caretaker. He was the man who had always called me "Donnie" back in the old neighborhood - the Cigar himself. So I turned to him and said, "Yes."

"I want to talk to you," he said.

"That's what I heard," I said.

And so we talked. The Cigar enquired after my mother who was suffering terribly from a brain tumor and who would die shortly thereafter. He was truly concerned about her. And then we talked about old times in the neighborhood, but my mind was still spinning a hundred miles a minute. What is this favor he wants, I wondered. What is he going to ask me to do? What can he possibly want from me, and why is he planting flowers in October, and . . .

"Donnie," he said, "I want a favor."

Time stood still. When I got my tongue working again, I said: "Well, I'll be happy to do anything

I can for you. You know that, just for old time's sake, if nothing else, and just out of sheer respect. And you know this is a second-generation friendship."

Just like that. I paused for breath, and then I added: "What is it? What can I do?"

I didn't think he wanted to borrow money from my bank or ask me to do anything illegal, but still...

So I was wanting him to hurry up and tell me what he wanted. End the suspense already! But the Cigar moved at his own speed, and he finally said with concern clearly showing on his face: "I want you to do me a favor, a very important favor to me."

I would come to find out just why he was so concerned, and so will you, but now you will hear him say: "I know since you bought the bank that you've been cleared by the FBI, the National Bank Examiner, and the National Controller of Currency."

How he knew all that, I'll never know, but I wasn't about to ask. Suffice it to say that when an Italian from Chicago bought a bank in those days, the feds got mighty nosey and left no drawer unturned.

So I told the Cigar that it was true that I had been thoroughly investigated by the federal government and found to be as clean as they come. But I couldn't help asking: "But what's that got to do with meeting me here today?"

The man I had mistaken for a cemetery caretak-

er looked me in the eyes and said: "I need somebody clean who I can trust; somebody I've known
all my life."

I qualified on all counts, so I blurted: "Well,
what is it? Tell me! The curiosity is killing me."

"I want you to do me a favor. I want you to
become Alderman of the First Ward of the City of
Chicago. I don't want you to do anything illegal,
and you will never be asked to do anything illegal."

But the First Ward was notorious for certain
nefarious activities, so I asked the Cigar: "But what
about all the gambling that goes on in that ward."

His answer was simple: "Just ignore it."

I could finally take a normal breath.

CHAPTER SEVEN

THE FIRST WARD
(A WORLD OF ITS OWN)

Sam Giancana might as well have asked me to be crowned the King of England as to be elected Alderman of the First Ward of Chicago.

Why? Because when I said in the last chapter that a certain ward was responsible for putting John F. Kennedy in the White House in 1960, I was referring to the one and only First Ward.

Forget about crowning kings, the First Ward, with its mere 30,000 voters, got to determine the course of history in 1960 by giving Joe Kennedy's boy the margin of victory he needed over Richard "Tricky Dick" Nixon.

I will reveal how it all came down at the end of this chapter, but I want to begin by holding up a mirror of America - the First Ward. It housed the seats of city and county government and had a huge federal presence in the courts and government offices on Dearborn. Why they even built the Metropolitan Correctional Center on Van Buren and opened it in 1975 as a service to the nearby federal courts.

The First Ward, with its bus and train stations, was the port of entry for countless people coming to Chicago for the first time. They had heard wonderful stories about Chicago, and they were seeing upon arrival in the First Ward that the city of big shoulders had skyscrapers to rival New York and a lakefront second to none.

What other city has beautiful parks and gardens right in the middle of its central business district? You look out the window of an office building in the First Ward and you see the green of Grant Park and the blue waters of Lake Michigan. No other city I can think of has a front yard like Chicago does with its First Ward.

The State of Illinois had offices on LaSalle, and all the fine hotels were in the First Ward. One of them, the Sherman House, served as an unofficial city hall, sitting as it did right across the street from the actual city hall.

You had your big department stores on State Street like Marshall Field's and Carson Pirie Scott. Families from all over the Chicago area flocked to Marshall Field's at Christmas to have breakfast under the tree in the Walnut Room and to see the "real" Santa Claus.

There was a time when you dressed up to go downtown to the First Ward and eat in the fancy restaurants and take in a show at such grand old

theaters as the Chicago or the State. Both the
Chicago Symphony Orchestra and the Lyric Opera
perform in the First Ward, and those lions guard-
ing the Art Institute of Chicago on Michigan
Avenue have long been a symbol of the power that
presides in the First Ward of Chicago.

There, among its 30,000 voters, you would
have found Italians, African-Americans, Poles, Bohemians, Chinese, and the Jews and Gypsies who
ran the world-famous Maxwell Street Market.

The whole world came to Maxwell Street in its
day because those mainly Jewish merchants would
sell you anything and everything at the lowest
prices anywhere, seven days a week, rain or shine.

Maxwell Street made many a merchant rich, and
two of the most famous were United States Supreme Court Justice Arthur Goldberg and the man
who could play "the licorice stick" like no one else,
Benny Goodman.

Maxwell Street was a magnet for bargain hunt-
ers, attracting hundreds of thousands of visitors
every year. There were so many people on Maxwell
Street on market days that you couldn't fall over if
you tried.

And the attraction was that the merchants
wanted you to believe that they were dealing in
"hot" goods. They weren't "hot" goods; they were
"cold" goods that they got from close-outs and
stores that wanted to unload inferior merchandise
that wasn't moving, cheap.

I know all about Maxwell Street because we had
a city payroller in the First Ward whose actual title

was "The Market Master." His job was to see that you got a better stand location for a slight consideration over the usual 17 cents a day it cost to operate on Maxwell Street.

The Market Master was backed up by the "Captain's Man," who, of course, represented the local police district.

The Captain's Man's pockets were never empty, because he collected a quarter every day from every merchant on the street as his "collection fee." For a quarter a day, the merchants got the privilege of being left alone by the police.

But far and away the most lucrative player on Maxwell Street was one Bennie "the Book."

You would set up your stand, make a few sales, and then along would come Bennie "the Book" to take your "bets" on whatever was running or playing that day. Mostly it was the horses, but Bennie could make book on just about anything. Bennie saved you a trip to the track, and he'd promptly pay you if and when you won.

The wonderful world of Maxwell Street got shoved aside by the University of Illinois, Chicago Circle Campus. But I am happy to report that the city has at least tried to honor the spirit of the old Maxwell Street Market by closing off Canal Street on Sundays and allowing merchants to sell food and goods there. It's worth checking out any Sunday between 7 a.m. and 3 p.m., but old-timers like me won't mistake it for the real thing.

The real Maxwell Street Market is gone, and I remember its "funeral" which came in the form of the dedication of the University of Illinois' Chicago Circle Campus.

Three officials were invited to make speeches at the dedication: Illinois Governor Otto Kerner, Chicago Mayor Richard J. Daley, and yours truly, the newly minted Alderman of the mighty First Ward of Chicago.

No one ever believed that the First Ward Alderman would be making a speech at a university, but there I was, exercising my golden tongue.

In chapter 2 you read all about my old neighborhood on Taylor Street, "Little Italy." Well, let me tell you: Little Italy was a big player in First Ward politics, because the Italians had the most votes in the ward and we delivered them.

Little Italy was and still is predominantly Italian, and you will still find Italians living side-by-side with the Chinese in Chinatown. That harmonious relationship began when Italian politicians overlooked the Chinese opium dens and gambling operations they called "Barbuet." And long before anyone was talking about racial harmony, the Italians of Little Italy were peacefully coexisting with their black neighbors in the housing projects that the city had built on the west side of their neighborhood.

There was never any racial tension, but I often think that was because the Italians had the guns and the African-Americans did not.

And so, as we continue our tour of the fabled old First Ward of Chicago, we find a Polish/Bohemian enclave called "Pilsen" that was centered around 18th and Halsted.

The Poles and Bohemians are wonderful, hard-working people who keep their property as good looking as the day it was built. But when I ran for Alderman, they were being replaced by a growing population of Hispanics who actively campaigned against me.

Head just north of old Pilsen under the railroad viaduct at 15th Street and you would have found a vibrant Produce Market that attracted grocers from as far away as Michigan. It was really something to see and hear what with trucks coming and going and people unloading boxes of the best vegetables and fruit you could find anywhere.

The First Ward extended over to the lakefront where, of course, the Chicago Tribune's legend-in-his-own-mind, Colonel Robert R. McCormick, had no objection whatsoever to having a convention center named in his honor. The Colonel always said the lakefront should remain unspoiled for all to enjoy, but how could he refuse a "little" lakefront convention center called McCormick Place?

Now, when I said the First Ward was "fabled," I was thinking all the way back to the days of a certain high-class entertainment venue immediately south of the Loop called the Everleigh Club.

The "club" was operated by the prim and proper Everleigh sisters who listed the captains of Chicago commerce as their patrons. And let the record show that Marshall Field, the famous real estate developer and department store owner, was caught with his pants down in there one night.

The Everleigh Club goes back to the wild days of the Lords of the Levee when the legendary Michael "Hinky Dink" Kenna and "Bathhouse" John Coughlin ruled their free-wheeling domaine south of the Loop as the two Aldermen of the First Ward.

That's right, each ward had two aldermen in those days, and the First Ward had the picks of the litter in those two Irish crime bosses. Hinky Dink and Bathhouse John were truly "Lords of the Levee" for a good 50 years, and I recommend, for your further reading, the excellent book of the same title by Lloyd Wendt and Herman Kogan. It's available on Amazon.com, and, like this book, it will keep you up late at night flipping from one chapter to the next.

When the Lords of the Levee left this mortal coil, the Chicago Outfit naturally stepped in to keep the legends of the Levee alive. But we have to head back downtown to the Loop itself to find the real romance of the First Ward.

The Loop, or course, gets its name from its famous circle of elevated rapid transit tracks, and it draws a million or more people on any given day. Half come to work, and the other half come to shop or visit the museums and cultural attractions, and the number increases in the summer when the tourists pour into Chicago.

The Loop always consisted of high-rise office buildings with a cigar stand in every lobby. And in every cigar stand would be, you guessed it - a bookmaker.

They used to say that if you operated a book joint in the Loop for a year you could clear a cool $1 million in profits. That sounds a little high to me, but then you should have seen some of the bets those good, honest office workers were making in those days.

A million or more people filled the Loop every day during the day, but we claimed only 30,000 actual voters. And of that 30,000, at least 8,000 were on a payroll with either the city, the state, the county, or the Municipal Employees Union.

The First Ward controlled the latter, so we got to decide who got placed in private industry. And each job that we put out was worth at least three votes. So we would have 24,000 votes to cast as we saw fit.

We were truly an invincible political machine. And the First Ward really flexed its political muscles in November 1960 when it put John F. Kennedy in the White House.

And they did it the old-fashioned way by controlling 12 other wards, or "controllable votes."

We didn't "count" votes in those days, we "weighed" them, meaning we could easily switch at least 80 percent of those votes to "our" candidate.

The First Ward also controlled five Italian aldermen, two non-Italian aldermen, and the five black wards in United States Congressman William "Bill" Dawson's district. The Outfit had taken control of the good Congressman by cutting him in on the Numbers Racket that was so popular with his constituents.

So we have set the stage for one of the closest elections in American history, the November 1960 contest between the Catholic Kennedy and the Quaker Nixon. The eyes of the nation were focused inward at Chicago and the First Ward in particular, because that's where the deciding votes would be cast.

But everybody had to go to bed that night not knowing who was going to succeed Eisenhower as 35th President of the United States of America.

And the country was still holding its breath by 10 o'clock Chicago time the next morning. Why?

Because we knew that if we stole all those votes and Kennedy lost anyway, Richard Nixon would have retaliated by appointing a Republican District Attorney for Chicago who would surely have indicted anyone caught stealing votes.

So we waited until we were absolutely certain that Kennedy would carry the day before sending word to the wards we controlled: "Kennedy's in! Kennedy has carried Illinois."

John F. Kennedy, son of bootlegger Joe Kennedy, would become the next President of the United States. And this despite the oppositions own considerable wheeling and dealing.

Don't forget, we're talking about old Tricky Dick Nixon here, and Nixon, being Nixon, he had persuaded Democratic delegates in key southern states to break ranks and vote for him, not the Catholic with the silver spoon in his mouth.

So Illinois was absolutely crucial to Kennedy's victor. And no part of Illinois was more crucial than the fabled First Ward of Chicago.

So the First Ward sent the word out to the other wards that Kennedy had carried Illinois by about 8,800 votes. We had to make sure that the win was by more than 5,000 votes because the law at the time required an automatic recount for anything less than that. And Kennedy's running mate, good old Lyndon B. Johnson, put his Texas political machine to work by ensuring that Kennedy took not only the Lone Star State but Missouri. LBJ's Texas machine was second only to Chicago's, and he used it to good effect in 1960.

When Nixon learned later that morning that he had lost Missouri, he knew he had lost the election.

It was official: John F. Kennedy would be our next President.

And I would have been in the catbird's seat had I but said "yes" to Sam "the Cigar" Giancana.

But I said, "No."

CHAPTER EIGHT

FROM VICTORY IN WEST VIRGINIA TO
DEATH IN DALLAS
(A NEW POLITICAL BARRIER IS BROKEN)

Can a Catholic win in the South? That was the question facing John F. Kennedy long before he could count on the First Ward to help him become the thirty-fifth President of the United States in November 1960.

And Kennedy's first big test came in the notoriously anti-Catholic state of West Virginia. He had just edged out Minnesota's liberal Senator, Hubert "Happy Warrior" Humphrey, in the Wisconsin primary by taking six of the state's ten Congressional districts.

But it wasn't the big win he was expecting, so he and his advisors put all their hopes on West Virginia. It was win West Virginia, or withdraw from the race. And West Virginia voters were faced with two slices from the same ultra-liberal loaf, the only difference being that Kennedy was an East Coast Catholic, and Humphrey was a Midwest Protestant.

And both campaigns were pouring money into the state, so voters were having a heck of a time deciding. But then what always decides an election? The almighty dollar.

Humphrey had the backing of the legitimate labor unions and he funneled their generous contributions into his West Virginia campaign, even though it was against the law.

But Kennedy had a bigger war chest in the form of Sam "the Cigar" Giancana and the Chicago Outfit, and so he was able to outspend Humphrey five-to-one. The Cigar's backing paid off with Kennedy beating Humphrey in West Virginia by 84,000 votes. No Catholic could have ever expected to take West Virginia, but Kennedy, with the Cigar's backing, had done it.

From there it was on to California where Kennedy clinched the nomination of the Democratic Party. And, as I said in the last chapter, he was faced with a formidable opponent in the form of Richard M. Nixon, aka Tricky Dick.

It was nip and tuck from the start, with polls showing Nixon up one day and Kennedy ahead the next day. Pundits said it was going to be too close to call, and they were certainly right when Kennedy won the popular vote by only 100,000.

But, as with every Presidential election, it was the Electoral College that put Kennedy in the White House.

John F. Kennedy was happy to be elected President of the United States, but his father, Ambassador Joe Kennedy, was even happier. The old bootlegger had put his Irish-Catholic boy in the White House.

But the Cigar was the happiest of all, because as he said to me, "Donny, did you ever think I'd elect a guy President of the United States?"

So let's look back at West Virginia and see what turned the election for Kennedy there. Was it his political philosophy? His good looks and mane of red hair? His golden tongue?

None of the above.

And both Kennedy and Humphrey were spending vast sums of money in West Virginia, because they both knew it was the show-down state. As I said, Kennedy outspent Humphrey big time, but he also put his money where it would do the most good, in the pockets of the real political bosses - the county sheriffs.

And taking as they did money from the Chicago Outfit and the rest of the Organized Crime Syndicate, those political operatives in West Virginia knew it was in their best interests to deliver the agreed number of votes.

Sure, they took money from Humphrey too, but they pocketed that as chump change. Kennedy's campaign was the real game, because, after all, his old man had been associated with Organized Crime most of his life.

And Kennedy's West Virginia workers were no altar boys themselves, having had extensive dealings with local gangsters. So they happily took Kennedy's big money and delivered the votes they had promised.

They got their money, but they also got something even better, their kind of man in the White House. And that leads us to just what kind of President of the United States John F. Kennedy would become.

After pouring all that money into Kennedy's victory over Nixon, the Cigar and his partners in organized crime were expecting some pretty big pay-offs, particularly ridding Cuba of that pest, Fidel Castro. They wanted to get that gold mine 90 miles from Florida going again, and Jack Kennedy was supposed to be the man to do it.

Well, a year passed with no return on their 1960 investment. The Cigar was not a happy camper, nor were any of the other bosses in New York and elsewhere. They had showed Kennedy the money, and he was showing no sign of running Castro out of Cuba. And then, when he finally launched the totally botched Bay of Pigs operation in 1961, he was responsible for getting more well-intentioned Cuban patriots killed in one day than the Chicago Outfit had given Taylor Street Justice to in its entire history.

Kennedy had promised that his Bay of Pigs plan would work, and the Cigar had thus told the other bosses to be patient. Give it time. All will be well.

Well, it wasn't, was it?

And, if you ask me, I would say that our tobacco companies had as much to say about the planning of the Bay of Pigs invasion as the crime syndicates.

After all, the price of a good cigar in America today is more than $5. If Cuba was able to import their even better cigars, you'd be paying somewhere in the neighborhood of $1 for one terrific smoke.

When the Cigar asked what the hold up was, Kennedy said Khrushchev and the Russians were putting Cuba under their umbrella and that he had to keep his hands off Castro and company.

But that was just another farce perpetuated by the Kennedys on the Cigar.

But Kennedy finally did authorize the disastrous Bay of Pigs operation in 1961, ensuring that those brave Cuban exiled rebels were slaughtered on the beach without effective air and naval support.

They had been trained and supplied by the Kennedy Administration, and Kennedy acknowledged full responsibility for the fiasco. But it was a good eight months before Kennedy finally realized what the consequences of his blunder were.

Frankly, I don't think he ever knew how big a problem he really had.

The Cigar didn't give up hope after the Bay of Pigs. He still thought Kennedy might deliver, but he was under a lot of pressure, because the other outfits around the country were demanding to know when they were finally going to get Cuba back.

They had invested big money in Kennedy, and he was failing to deliver. Kennedy kept putting the Cigar off, and in late 1962 he really did have a big problem with the Russians in the form of the Cuban Missile Crisis.

The U.S. Navy was intercepting Russian ships on the high seas, and people were lined up around the block at Saint Peters Catholic Church in the Loop waiting to confess their sins before the end of the world.

It was that serious, but Kennedy told the Cigar not to worry because the Russians were really turning their ships back before they could deliver their missiles to Cuba. It was all a big farce, Kennedy said.

But if that was true, then whoever perpetrated such a farce should be shot. And, sure enough, they were both shot later on.

While Cuba was boiling over on the front burner, those skirt-chasing Kennedy boys were having their own little personal crisis on the back burner with one Marilyn Monroe.

Seems that Bobby Kennedy just happened to have paid the blonde bombshell a visit hours before she was murdered. Oops! So Bobby and his big brother Jack called the Cigar for help.

Marilyn Monroe, it seemed, had secretly photographed her little dalliance with Bobby, and she was threatening to blackmail the Kennedys if they didn't take care of her the way she wanted.

Born Norma Jeane Mortenson on June 1, 1926, Marilyn Monroe was the personification of Hollywood glamour by the time of her entanglement with the Kennedy brothers.

The official Marilyn Monroe website boldly

declares that "her apparent vulnerability and inno-
cence, in combination with an innate sensuality, has
endeared her to the global consciousness. She dominated the age of movie stars to become, without
question, the most famous woman of the 20th
Century."

Some of the most famous writers of the 20th
Century like Norman Mailer and Joyce Carol Oates
wrote books about Marilyn Monroe, and baseball
superstar Joe DiMaggio married her on January 14,
1954 at San Francisco's City Hall.

They divorced nine months later, and Marilyn
Monroe married playwright Arthur Miller on June
29, 1956. That marriage ended on January 20,
1961 when Marilyn was appearing in The Misfits
with Clark Gable and Montgomery Clift.

She won a Golden Globe for Best Actress in a
Comedy for her performance in the 1959 film,
Some Like It Hot. During her career, she made 30
films, and left one, Something's Got to Give, un-
finished. A global sensation, Marilyn Monroe was
named female World Film Favorite at the 1962
Golden Globes.

And, in August of that year, she thought she
had the Kennedy brothers just where she wanted
them with her evidence of their affairs with her.

Who better than the President of the United
States and his brother, the Attorney General of the
United States, to advance an aging starlet's career?

So the Kennedys made an urgent call to the
Cigar who reached out to certain contacts in California who in turn sent a certain "messenger of

death" to see Marilyn Monroe that very evening at her home in Brentwood.

The official reports said Marilyn Monroe "died in her sleep," but the fact was that Marilyn's big red lips were sealed forever, and the Kennedys' embarrassing little problem was solved. But they owed the Cigar and the Outfit big time, so they promised a Castro-free Cuba and exclusive gambling rights as the payoff.

Enter the Cuban Missile Crisis, and President Kennedy was suddenly not returning phone calls from Chicago. After Kennedy supposedly turned the Russian ships back in late 1962, he ran out of excuses. It was obvious to everybody in the know that Kennedy had double-crossed the Cigar. He simply could not and would not deliver Cuba as promised. Which caused certain connected people to be very, very unhappy.

And it wasn't just organized crime that suffered when those Cuban exiles got gunned down at the Bay of Pigs. The CIA had their own horses in that race, and they were not happy to see Fidel Castro remain in power.

So this all leads to the $8 million question. Who killed John F. Kennedy on November 22, 1963 in Dallas, Texas?

You have your theories, and I have mine.

But I will tell you with absolute certainty that Kennedy did not get Taylor Street Justice, because the Chicago Outfit did not have any part of it.

And I will also tell you that nobody talks about Kennedy's assassination because there is no statute of limitations on murder.

Who in his right mind is going to brag that he shot the President of the United States?

But I have my doubts when it comes to the man who shot Lee Harvey Oswald on live television as Dallas police were moving their "number one suspect" out of their downtown jail. The Cigar always referred to Oswald as "that poor kid who was used as a patsy."

He would refer to Ruby, who was from Chicago, but he would never complete the story. Ruby, you see, owned some night clubs in New Orleans and was deeply in debt to the "juicemen" in the syndicate. Jack Ruby was one desperate character because, not only did he not have the wherewithal to pay back his "juice" loans, but he knew he was dying of cancer.

I think they arranged with Ruby to kill Lee Harvey Oswald in the Dallas jail two days after the assassination. I cannot substantiate my theory, but I have to ask how Ruby would have known that the Dallas police were going to move Oswald that day when they had never made a public announcement of their intentions? And why would somebody unlock the door and let Ruby in with a loaded gun?

Those essential questions remain unanswered to this day.

While I was never a great fan of the Kennedy clan, I had a tear in my eye when I heard John F. Kennedy was been killed in Dallas.

He was my President too.

Donnie Parrillo

CHAPTER NINE

"NO" THEN "YES"
(A CALL FROM BUDDY)

So what does a call from a character called Benjamin "Buddy" Jacobson, just two nights after my heart-stopping meeting with the Cigar at my father's grave, have to do with any of this?

Plenty. Buddy Jacobson, you see, was the guy the Cigar promised would give me a call after our little talk at the cemetery about me possibly running for First Ward Alderman. And Buddy wasn't some nobody that nobody sent. He was Secretary of the First Ward Regular Democratic Organization, and he earned an underworld Purple Heart by being one of the four met shot in front of Holy Name Cathedral during the Bootlegging Wars of the 1920s.

Buddy and three others were standing by the cathedral at the corner of State and Superior when gunmen from Dion O'Banion's Gang emptied their weapons at them. Two men died, and Buddy Jacobson was one of the two men who lived to tell about it. And what Buddy told me was that the first bullet hit him in the gut and knocked him into a deep gutter, with only his right leg showing. That's what saved him, and you can still see that high curb there today, but you won't find a plaque to mark the occasion.

You have to read my book to know that quite often Buddy would roll up his shirt and show off the scar where that first bullet hit him, and then he would roll up his pant leg to show you his shattered right leg. Those were his underworld Purple Heart Medals, and he was rightfully proud of them.

A product of the so-called Jewish "Gehenna" on the West Side, Buddy Jacobson was a true character from the rip-roarin' days of Prohibition that shows like "The Untouchables" can't even begin to touch. So I got the promised call from Buddy Jacobson himself, and, naturally, he wanted to know what he should tell the Cigar.

"You gonna run, or ain't you gonna run?" That was the question, and the Cigar was eager to hear my answer.

So I told Buddy that, yes, I would really enjoy doing the Cigar a favor. And I told him that, having grown up in a political environment, I would certainly enjoy being First Ward Alderman.

But I had to say, "No thank you." No, because being Alderman would take too much time away from my business.

But the main reason was that I had a new, young

bride at the time, and she was totally opposed to any involvement in politics. Buddy heard me out, and then he patiently explained that the Cigar was not going to like my answer.

"Nobody turns this guy down," he said.

"Yeah," I said. "Well, tell him I'm sorry. I hope to see him in the near future, but there is nothing I can do about it right now."

"Well, I'll bring the message back, but he's not going to like it." That was that, but then Buddy called the very next day to say, "Look at it this way. You'll make so much damn money and get so many bank accounts that you will be more than happy you took the job. And if your wife is your only problem, here's what the Cigar told me to tell you." I was all ears, so he asked if she was Irish.

"Yes, she is."

"Good," he said. "That means she must like to drink. So what is her favorite restaurant?"

"That private dining club on the near North Side - the Whitehall." It was probably the best restaurant in all of Chicago, so naturally it was her favorite.

So Buddy said: "Okay, here's what the Cigar said to do. Take your wife out to dinner tomorrow night at the Whitehall. There won't be any check for you. Everything is going to be taken care of. The Cigar said to load her up with champagne and wine - whatever she likes to drink. Get her good and juiced, and then take her home. After that, put her in bed, and jump her. And while you're jumping her say, 'Could I run for First Ward Alderman?', and she will say yes. Guaranteed!"

So I dutifully took my Irish wife to her favorite restaurant the following night, and when we pulled up in front of the Whitehall, two snappy valets were waiting to take my car. We walked in and ate and drank our fill, and, yes, I made sure that my wife's glass was never empty.

And then when I went to pay the check, they said it was taken care of. When I tried to tip our waiter, he said that was taken care of too. And I didn't need to tip the captain or the maitre 'd, because somebody had taken care of that too. And not only was my car waiting for us when we emerged from the Whitehall, but we found that it had been washed and polished. I was starting to get a little taste of just how much influence the Cigar had on every phase of my life.

Having eaten and drunk our fill, my wife and I went home for a night of love. And so, during the throes of passion, I popped the big question: "Honey, I would really like to run for First Ward Alderman. Is it all right with you?"

And she said, "Yes."

And so I was not surprised when the phone rang at 4 a.m. that very morning, and the caller was none other than Buddy Jacobson wanting to know if the plan had worked.

Without bothering to say hello, I said: "Tell the Cigar he's got a candidate."

Buddy said the Cigar would be pleased to know and that my intentions would be strictly on the QT until late in December 1963 when I would have to file my nominating petition. And I didn't want any press until then, because I knew such "adverse publicity" could only hurt deposits at my bank. But I also figured that I would regain those deposits right after I had won the election.

We agreed that I would campaign as a candidate who "was pure as the new fallen snow," and that any dirty work would be done by the Cigar's friends.

So there I was, ready to jump into public life and possibly become Alderman of the most powerful political entity in the country, the First Ward of Chicago. I was excited, because it was an exciting time. I mean, how many people get an opportunity like that in life? Precious few, that's for sure. So with my head filled with grand political possibilities, I took my wife on a ski vacation in November to our home in Vail, Colorado. The lift wasn't running yet, but there was enough snow, so we made our usual arrangement to have them take us halfway up the mountain in a private jeep and then ski down. We'd do that eight or ten times a day.

And it was while we were skiing in Vail that I got a call from Buddy who told me I had to get back to Chicago, immediately! My wife was none too happy about that and certainly didn't want to cut our vacation short on account of some "Big Shot's call," but I told her if Buddy said it was important we get back, then we had to hop the next flight.

Buddy, of course, was absolutely right, because I was whisked from O'Hare to First Ward Democratic Headquarters where the political heavyweights were waiting for me. After we exchanged pleasantries, Buddy took me for a walk down La-Salle Street so we could talk in private.

"What's the big rush here?" I asked.

"Listen," Buddy said, "something came up, and the Cigar wants you to announce right away that you're going to be a candidate for alderman. They've got a very big problem, because they have something on him. So he wants to get rid of it before anything goes wrong."

Being from the old neighborhood, I had learned not to ask, so I didn't ask what the Cigar's problem was. But I did call a press conference for November 21, 1963 and announced that I was a candidate for First Ward Alderman.

The very next day, November 22, 1963, President John F. Kennedy was assassinated.

Don skiing with Governor William G. Stratton of Illinois in Sun Valley, Idaho.

CHAPTER TEN

THE CAMPAIGN
("AH, DEMOCRACY! I LOVE IT!")

I launched my campaign for Alderman of the First Ward with a mass meeting of some 2,500 supporters in a downtown hall. There were county, city and state workers, plus bookmakers and people obligated to the Outfit. In other words, people who depended on the First Ward for a living.

Looking out at the multitude, I saw every ethnic and economic class, and, yes, there were some wealthy bookmakers among them.

The United States Congressman for that district began the testimonials on my behalf with these words: "We're now about to honor the prominent son of a prominent father, who has been a very dear and close friend of my father's for years."

I later learned that the Congressman would never be running again for re-election, hence the Cigar's aforementioned problem.

Then two Illinois State Senators spoke on my behalf, followed by two State Representatives. They called several precinct captains to the microphone, and everybody told everybody there what a wonderful human being I was. (I like to think I still am.)

For me the funniest moment of the night occurred when a speaker introduced the head of the Municipal Employees' Union as a "friend of the poor."

I laugh even now as I picture that "friend of the poor" with an enormous diamond rock on his hand that took two hands to hold up and a thousand-dollar suit. But it was even funnier when he said: "You can't trust these newspapers. All of our guys are out on the streets working like dogs. They stop for one minute to take a piss, and they're on page one of the Chicago papers. But that's not fair."

Then he added: "The owners of those newspapers are all those rich bastards sitting on their yackets (he meant yachts). They don't care about the poor people. We do, and that's why we have to elect this guy as the next Alderman of the First Ward."

Every TV station in the Midwest was there, and a New York paper even sent a reporter to cover it. It was a classic for sure, and you'll never see a night like that again.

After that rousing start to my campaign, I took to the streets and made every civic luncheon and dinner, went to all the churches and met all the pastors, black as well as white.

And when I campaigned in Chinatown, I made the mistake of saying: "I want to thank all you Chinamen who came to hear me tonight." I was later chastised for calling them "Chinamen" and was told that was akin to calling an Italian a "dago."

But those good Chinese-American voters did applaud me for what I was going to do for them when elected, which was chiefly to ignore their opium dens and "barbuet" gambling operations.

I also appeared on every radio and television talk show, and I appeared on the two late night shows several times.

Why did they want me? Because this was the first time in Chicago history that a First Ward candidate was laying it all on the table. They had already scrupulously examined my background and found me to be in perfect order.

I didn't mind, because I had nothing to hide.

But for a while I thought of myself as more of an entertainer than a politician. I was on TV every night, on almost every channel. I was looking at a camera my every waking moment. I would start the day by having breakfast with a reporter at my home and then have them bird dog me for the rest of the day. Reporters followed me to the bank, they had lunch with me, and they even followed me out to River Forest for my visits to my ailing mother. She was seriously ill at the time, so I had dinner with her almost every night.

The "fair" news media covered everything I did and didn't do, and they never gave me the benefit of the doubt. And these were the same "objective reporters" who had endorsed John F. Kennedy for President in 1960 when he was 40 and had never earned a penny on his own.

Never mind that I was already a self-made millionaire by the time I was 33, and better educated than Kennedy. And I'm sure my standard of morality was much higher than his. Yet half the media said Kennedy was qualified to be President of the United States, but that I was "not qualified" to be Alderman of the First Ward.

Ah, I love that media. Really, I do.

Anyway, elections in the First Ward were normally automatic. Sure, they would sometimes put up one candidate against another just to raise money, and then, when they got the dough, they would have the first candidate withdraw. But this was to be the first election in the history of the First Ward to be fought on the level, because the FBI was all over every precinct. This was the first time we were going to have real opposition.

Also, we were one of three wards running in the Special Election of 1964, and the other two wards' candidates were to be elected automatically. Meaning that the media and the anti-administration organizations turned out in force to oppose me. And to top that off, they donated tons of money to my opponent, a lovely lady from the old Taylor Street neighborhood named Florence Scala.

Her platform was simply that the University of Illinois had displaced some 10,000 Italian voters. She numbered many of them among her personal friends and was counting on their support for victory in the election.

So I had my work cut out for me as I began my campaign and found that my opponent had more supporters at local meetings than I did. But the older timers said: "Don't worry about it; she's not going anywhere."

But I was worried because the winds of reform were blowing across the country, and the First Ward was feeling it the most. We could have turned out 24,000 votes, but everybody agreed we did not want to give me an overwhelming victory.

So, we agreed that I would get about 8,000 votes and give her about 1,000 to make it look like it was a "real" election. Well, we tried to do exactly that, but my opponent actually got 3,000 votes. Everybody was stunned, because that was unheard of in the First Ward.

I visited every precinct in the First Ward on Election Day, and when I got to the projects in the black area, I found a precinct captain passing out money to every voter.

So I said: "Once they take your money, how do you know that they're still going to vote for me?"

The precinct captain replied: "These black bastards don't get a vote. I hand them this card, which reads, 'I cannot read or write. I wish to cast my vote for Donald W. Parrillo, Alderman of the First Ward in the City of Chicago.'"

The voter, according to the precinct captain, would then hand his card to the Judge of the Election (who we controlled), and the judge would

*Headlines and reports from Donnie Parrillo's victory over
Mrs. Scala in the First Ward.
To better view the articles please visit our website at
www.caponemaygofree.com.*

Parrillo Defeats
Mrs. Scala 3-1;

Opposing the West Side housewife in the 1st Ward alder-
manic election, 33-year-old banker Donald W. Parrillo votes
with his wife Nancy. (Sun-Times Photos)

WEATHER:
Partly cloudy and mild
Wednesday with a high in
the 50s. See Page 46.

CHICAGO
SUN-TIMES

© 1964 by Field Enterprises, Inc.

FINAL
HOME EDITION

Vol. 16, No. 304.

Phone 321-3000

WEDNESDAY, JANUARY 22, 1964

68 Pages—7 Cents

Parrillo Defeats Mrs. Scala

3-1; Danaher Sweeps

go and pull the lever for him. We were pulling the lever for everybody in the Ward, which meant that the so-called "voter" never did get to vote.

And to grease the skids for my victory, we had given the black ministers a hundred bucks a piece a few days before the election. But one pastor had a bigger flock than the others, so we gave him $200, and that was not lost on the other ministers.

Seeing that we had a real fight on our hands, they demanded more money for delivering their votes, and the minister with the biggest following demanded $1,000. Another guy wanted $500.

We were absolutely counting on the black vote for victory, so we resolved the problem the Taylor Street way.

Certain people called on the minister asking for the big bucks, and they put a .45-caliber pistol in his mouth, and gave him $50. That's all it took for him to be "for" Donald W. Parrillo for Alderman.

The minister who wanted $500 got a beating, and no one has seen or heard from him since that day, but, in the end, his congregation was "for" me too.

We also had trouble with a newly organized Hispanic group that opposed my election. Of the group's three main leaders, one was a businessman who had about 30 juke boxes in Hispanic taverns around the city, the second owned a big restaurant in their neighborhood, and the third man owned a weekly Hispanic newspaper that blasted me every issue.

We did not want the Spanish to establish a

foothold in the First Ward, so certain people took certain steps including the removal and destruction of 15 of those aforementioned juke boxes.

That Hispanic businessman and his organization suddenly decided that Donald W. Parrillo was the best candidate for Alderman of the First Ward. Then the Health Department closed down the second leader's restaurant for "flagrant violations," and, by the time he was able to reopen, he was firmly on my bandwagon. And, wouldn't you know, the Hispanic newspaper that was crusading against me suddenly had a bad fire and couldn't publish a word until after the election. But the publisher changed his tune and put signs for me around his neighborhood.

Such things may never occur again in American history, but they certainly did in 1964 in the First Ward of Chicago.

I spent Election Night in headquarters awaiting the returns. As I said, my opponent was supposed to only get 1,000 votes. So, when the final tabulation showed her with more than 3,000 votes, all the old-timers were shocked. Nobody but nobody could do that to the almighty First Ward Democratic Organization. So while everybody was celebrating my victory in song and dance, I leaned back in my chair and realized that I was witnessing the beginning of the end of the last political machine in America.

Ah, Democracy! I love it!

Needless to say, nobody bothered to oppose me when I ran for re-election. And so it was many years later that I found myself driving my 19-year-old son Timothy north on Michigan Avenue. He was an idealistic student at Ball State University in Muncie, Indiana at the time and so he was curious about the ways of Chicago politics.

So I pointed to an old hotel at the corner of 9th and Michigan and said: "Timothy, you see that building there?" He did. So I added: "When I ran for office, I would get 400 votes out of that building."

My son very naively said to me, "Gee, Dad, that building doesn't look big enough for 400 people to live in."

To which I replied: "Tim, I didn't say anybody actually lived there. I just said I'd get 400 votes out of that building. Actually, nobody lived there. That hotel has been shuttered for 25 or 30 years."

I didn't like shattering his illusions of the Great Democracy he had been taught in school, but I had to tell him the absolute truth, and I did.

And here are three stories to further illustrate my love of Democracy:

First, shortly after I was elected Alderman of the First Ward. I was asked by the people who lived in the projects to join them for a banquet honoring one of the greatest track stars in history, Jesse Owens. They wanted me to introduce him, and I gladly accepted. I loved having meals with my friends in the projects because they always fed me the best southern-fried chicken in the world, and I was especially honored to have been asked to introduce the legendary Olympian Jesse Owens.

So I prepared for the big night by thoroughly researching Jesse Owen's athletic achievements at the Chicago Public Library. I was ready to give him a proper introduction, and when the time came, I drove myself to the projects without a police bodyguard. These were my constituents, and I did not need protection when visiting them.

Well, I gave Jesse Owens just the great introduction that he deserved, and when I was done, he stood up and said it was the finest he had ever received, except that I had made one mistake - he had triumphed at the Olympics in Moscow, not Berlin as I had said. But, as he was speaking, I knew that couldn't be right, because I had done my homework at the library. So I went back to the books the next morning, and, sure enough, I found I had been right - Jesse Owens was the hero of the Berlin Olympics, not in Moscow as he had said. I don't know why Jesse changed it from Berlin to Moscow, but I always kidded him about it afterwards, whenever I saw him at other events.

Ah, Democracy! I love it!

And then, after I had been Alderman for a little longer time, Mayor Richard J. Daley introduced an ordinance to vacate an alley between the old Morrison Hotel and the future First National Bank building without bothering to tell me. So I told the Alderman who headed the committee that handled such matters that I would move to defer and publish it when it came up for a vote.

When an Alderman moves to defer and publish, all a second Alderman has to say is "I second the motion." That automatically defers the vote until the next regular council meeting. But we were about to adjourn for the summer, and the Mayor wanted to get it out of the way.

So when I walked into City Hall that morning, the Alderman who chaired that committee said His Honor wanted to see me in his office before the start of the council meeting. I dutifully reported to the Office of the Mayor on the fifth floor where Mayor Daley underscored the importance of the First National Bank to Chicago and demanded to know why I was objecting to his ordinance.

"My only objection," I said, "is that I am Alderman of this ward, and I was not told about this."

Mayor Daley remained seated and said he would appreciate it very much if I would just "let it go."

"I will not let it go," I said.

Richard J. Daley was famous for his temper, and he let me have a dose of it that morning as he rose from his chair and said: "If you don't let it go, I'll put a candidate against you in the next election."

I stood up and said, "Very well, Mr. Mayor, then you will have to find someone who wants to stand up and die."

We stood eyeball to eyeball for a moment, and then we both laughed and agreed to let Mayor Daley's ordinance go through.

Ah, Democracy! I love it!

Finally, here's a true tale of how two well-educated voters learned a real lesson in Chicago politics on election day:

Of the 60 precincts in the First Ward at the

time of my election, about two-thirds had voting machines and one-third still had paper ballots. The captains in those precincts with voting machines had keys to them. How they got them, I'll never know, but I do know they could open the machines and change the votes at will.

I made a point of visiting as many precincts as I could on election day, and I was having some homemade lasagna at one of the Italian precincts when in walks this well-dressed, well-educated woman who said she wanted to vote. No one knew who she was, so the so-called "independent" precinct committeeman shook his head from side to side and said he did not want this lady to vote.

The well-dressed woman insisted she was a registered voter and that she was going to cast her ballot that day. Well, we certainly knew that she was not going to cast her ballot that day for me, so the Judge of Elections asked her, "What is your name?"

I don't remember what she said, so for the sake of argument let's say she said: "Mary Smith."

The Judge of Elections then ran her finger up and down the polling sheets and said, "Mary Smith has already voted, and it is illegal to vote twice."

This Mary Smith became quite indignant and said, "I did not vote! I will go and get my husband and will be right back here, and I want to see you tell him that I already voted."

She huffed off, and I decided to stay and see the rest of the drama. Sure enough, she returned shortly with her well-dressed husband. He walked right up to the Judge of Elections and demanded, "Who said that my wife already voted? We just moved to the First Ward, and we want to vote, and I want to vote."

The Judge of Elections looked at him calmly and said, "What is your name?"

He said "John Smith" or something like it.

Then the Judge of Elections ran her finger up and down the polling sheets and said, "You already voted. You can't vote twice because it is illegal to vote twice."

Mr. Smith got all excited and threatened to go to the State's Attorney, the District Attorney, the Judge of Elections, the Cook County Judge of Elections - you name it - he was going to file complaints with them.

Little did Mr. Smith know that the Judge of the Precinct was the wife of a member of the Board of Elections. And every other place he threatened to go was occupied by people who had been put there with the First Ward's blessings. His protests would have truly fallen on deaf ears.

But time heals all wounds, because when I ran into that couple four years later, we had a friendly chat and they reported that they had voted for me.

Ah, Democracy! I love it!

Alderman Donald W. Parrillo at work.

Donnie Parrillo

CHAPTER ELEVEN

POWERFUL UNION
(UNION: POWER TO THE PEOPLE?)

The Chicago Outfit made their Hollywood debut in the late 1920s by taking over the Movie Union. They seized control from the legitimate businessmen who had started the union by telling them that it would be in there best interests to take a walk and not come back.

The Outfit thus became THE star machine, telling producers and directors who to cast and what pictures to make. And they were not reluctant to "suggest" their girlfriends for starring roles, regardless of their lack of talent and acting experience.

And the Outfit had the perfect Hollywood front man in industrialist/film producer Howard Hughes. One of the wealthiest people in the world, Hughes had found it profitable to do business with the Chicago Outfit, so he was happy to front for them as they seized control of the Union.

Hughes, after all, had benefited from the Outfit's ability to either break strikes at his plants or to keep the unions out all together. So he was happy to be seen with the beautiful women pushed his way like Jean Harlow. The press said she was Hughes' girlfriend, but Jean Harlow belonged to none other than Al Capone.

Only a select few had seen Jean Harlow with Capone in Chicago and on trains and other places, but the real proof of their relationship was the dose of fatal syphilis she gave Capone. But she also died of the same dreaded disease, and hospital officials would not disclose what had killed her.

But take it from me: Jean Harlow was the one who gave Al Capone syphilis. When Al Capone went to jail in 1931, Jean Harlow took up with one of the greatest actors of all time, William Powell.

He was famous for the "The Thin Man" series and starred in the Ziegfield Follies and many fine movies. Powell was at the top of his game when he suddenly disappeared from the silver screen for a year or so.

The official word was that he had rectal cancer, but what he really had was a case of syphilis he got from Jean Harlow. But timing was on his side, because medical advances enabled the doctors to save him.

Poor Al Capone just got his dose from Jean Harlow a little too early. William Powell regained his health and his career on the big screen, but poor Jean Harlow took a nose dive.

Word spread that she was suffering from syphilis, and her big shot boyfriends backed off in droves. Her career tanked, and she had to give up her fancy home near Hollywood and move back in with her mother. She died a lonely, abandoned woman with nothing to show for her time in Hollywood, save the ring William Powell had given her.

It was little wonder then that the Outfit wanted a plum like the Movie Union. Everybody and his brother loved the movies, and now the Outfit was going to decide exactly who and what got put up there on the silver screen.

They had power, prestige, and total creative control. Meaning that before any producer could make a movie, he had to pay the Union and give the Outfit their cut.

The producers were happy with this arrangement, because their payment to the Union's real bosses meant they would have absolutely no trouble making their pictures. No union problems, and they could get the stars of their choices. And who better to guarantee distribution than the Outfit? Only "their" pictures got shown in Chicago.

Just a minor coincidence, I suppose, that the Outfit also controlled the Movie Projectors Union, and that they could scotch the release of any "outlaw company's" film in other cities with a simple phone call to one of their crime syndicate contacts. It was a Hollywood movie come true! The producers were happy, the stars were happy, audiences got great movies as prices they could afford, and the Outfit was rolling in dough and dames.

But there is always one fly in every bowl of soup, and he proved to be the actor Robert Montgomery, who blew the whistle on the whole racket in 1943. Montgomery's testimony sent seven of the Outfit's top gangsters to prison on ten-year sentences.

But these were federal raps, and they were thus eligible for parole after serving only three and a third years of their sentences. And, wouldn't you know, U.S. Attorney General Tom Clark himself paroled them on the very day they were eligible, and told them to go home and behave themselves.

But they didn't. Two of the Hollywood Seven loudly complained that they hadn't gotten their fair share of the movie action. They had refused to take the witness stand and had served their time; now they wanted a bigger cut.

Those two whining wise guys made such a racket about the movie racket that the Outfit had no choice but to give them each a little Taylor Street Justice:

Charlie "Cherry Nose" Gio got whacked on Grand Avenue and his associate took his "Justice" in front of a club near Taylor Street itself.

Maybe they should have settled for not collecting their share of the movie money. But who am I to say?

But I do have more to say about the Outfit and Hollywood, because after Capone went to prison, they sent two other people to run the Movie

Union, under the auspices of Johnny Roselli, of whom you will read more shortly.

And who did the Outfit send? Willie Bioff, a Madison Street pimp with a terrible reputation, and a big fat guy named George E. Brown. The Outfit guys complained about the choice of Bioff, but the choice had been made by Frank Nitti, and he was the boss at the time.

So down come those aforementioned indictments in 1943, and who should appear as the government's star witness but Willie Bioff himself? Bioff copped a plea and was thus exonerated while the others went to prison.

I don't know what became of George E. Brown, but I do know that Willie Bioff moved to a small town in Arizona and lived quietly under the assumed name of "Willie Nelson" until the morning after those ten-year sentences had expired.

Thinking he was safe with his new name and identity, Willie opened his garage, climbed in his truck and fired it up.

"BOOM!"

He fired it up all right - all the way to the Pearly Gates where he may or may not have been admitted. That was the end of Willie Bioff, alias "Willie Nelson."

His body was so blown apart that when his wife went and talked to the police, she said: "Could you just find his ring or his watch to give me, please?"

The Outfit learned from the indictments that they needed to take a more sophisticated approach to Hollywood, and so they dispatched a young attorney named Sidney Korshak to direct the show.

Korshak was under the tutelage of this afore-mentioned Roselli, who was the Outfit's man in California. Having known him a long time ago, I can tell you that Johnny Roselli was a dapper, handsome man. I don't believe he ever married, but he dated every starlet who ever came from a small town in Texas to be discovered on the Great White Way of southern California.

I have my own Johnny Roselli story from the time a friend and I went to California to promote a character for a Christmas show. Roselli heard we were coming and had a limo waiting for us at the airport with a driver right out of a gangster movie. He was dressed in black with a white shirt, black tie, black hat, black gloves, and he was holding a sign reading: "Parrillo from Chicago."

He whisked us to the Beverly Hills Hotel and told us, he and the limo were at our disposal as long as we were in town. Well, we were in town to pitch this character we had created, and we wanted the people who owned the "Mr. Magoo" show to tell us if we had a winner on our hands.

While they were giving us excellent, profession-al advice, Jim Backus was in the next studio making a commercial for General Electric as Mr. Magoo.

The limo was waiting for us when we were done, and we had a great, three-day stay in California, with Johnny Roselli and company picking up the entire tab.

I had seen first-hand that the Outfit's powerful

tentacles reached far beyond Chicago to sunny southern California. And the Outfit octopus could put the squeeze on Hollywood, because they controlled the Union that controlled the making of every movie.

The Union, you see, was founded in the 1930s when almost all movies were made right on the "lot." And who better to control complete access to the lot, than the Union? But all that has changed. Most movies today are made on location with little or no shooting on lots.

The Union's power eroded, and those crafty producers began making their movies in cities where the Outfit had little or no influence. But that didn't stop the Outfit from waiting until a movie was about 90 percent finished before calling a strike. The producer learned that he had to pay up in order to put his film up on the silver screen.

But in the day, the Outfit could make anybody a star, even a skinny, ingrate, washed-up singer from Hoboken, New Jersey who they turned into the biggest star in show business.

Does "Old Blue Eyes" ring a bell? And, yes, you will read more about him later in this book. But now let's move on to another example of the Outfit's star-making power.

The scene is a relaxing Sunday afternoon in the home of the Paul "the Waiter" Ricca, Boss of the Chicago Outfit at the time. He was hosting card games in his recreation room. I was playing with some friends and Ricca's son, and the Waiter was playing poker at another table with five people.

A pleasant scene indeed, and periodically we could hear music and applause coming from the third floor of his three-story building. The Boss lived up there on the third floor, and his son lived on the second. The apartments were huge, and the building had an elevator.

So, after an hour of this, the Waiter's wife came into the rec room and said to her husband, "Papa?" He greeted her affectionately in Italian, saying: "Mama, ti voglio bene." That means, I love you very much, and he asked what he could do for her.

Well, she was accompanied by a handsome young man from Italy with a guitar strapped around his neck, so she said: "Oh, Papa, I just love this young man. He's got such a beautiful voice. Can you help him in his profession?"

And the Boss said to her: "Well, what does he want?"

She turned to the singer and said, "What do you want, young man?"

And he replied: "I'd like to be on the Ed Sullivan Show."

That was the show that Elvis Presley and the Beatles absolutely had to be on, because it was the hottest variety show in the country.

So Mrs. Ricca said to the young man: "When do you want to be on the show?"

"As soon as possible."

The Boss casually turned to the lawyer seated next to him and said, "Call the Jew in California and tell him to put this guy on the Ed Sullivan Show next Sunday."

Next Sunday, mind you, and we're talking about the most sought-after show in America. There's even a song about the Ed Sullivan Show in that popular musical, "Bye Bye, Birdie."

Well, I was glued to my set the following Sunday, and, sure enough, old Ed Sullivan himself says halfway through the show: "I'm now going to introduce you to a handsome young Italian - the greatest voice from Italy."

With Ed Sullivan's ringing endorsement and a last-minute booking on his show, the tenor from Cremona, Italy skyrocketed to fame and fortune.

His name? Sergio Franchi!

And here's a true story that goes to show how just much power the Outfit had over show business:

In 1963, Frank Sinatra, Dean Martin, and Sammy Davis Jr. put on a show for one week at a place called Villa Venice in the northwest suburbs of Chicago. It was a huge banquet hall that had long outlived its value, but in its heyday it featured a beautiful facade and gondolas plying the water that surrounded the building.

Many a fashionable wedding reception was held at the Villa Venice, and you had to book far in advance, because it was one classy place. They brought the Villa Venice back to life for that great event in 1963 and decorated every square inch of it.

Frank Sinatra, Dean Martin, and Sammy Davis Jr. were the triple crown of big-time entertainers in those days, and they were going to share the stage at the old Villa Venice in the Chicago suburbs, and the place had to look its best. And it did.

I did not go to the show, so I had one of my closest friends escort my wife who was anxious to see those three superstars perform together. She later commented that it was the greatest show she had ever seen. And the Cigar would often brag that he was the only guy powerful enough to "make" those three superstars appear on the same stage in some Chicago suburb when he "told them to".

And let the record show that shortly after this triumph that the Villa Venice burned to the ground under mysterious circumstances.

Need I say more about the power of the Outfit in the entertainment business?

CHAPTER TWELVE

CLAN KENNEDY
(FROM "JOE THE BOOTLEGGER"
TO "JOE THE AMBASSADOR")

*"If somebody made a decent living by violating
the Volstead Act, namely, 'Prohibition,' they
would call him 'Joe the Bootlegger.'
If somebody made $500 million by violating
the Volstead Act, they would call him
'Joe the Ambassador."* - Donnie Parrillo

I have nothing against the Kennedy family.
They are no better or worse than any other family
that has money and power. And I certainly have to
salute Joe Kennedy for being the most formidable
political power in the United States as "Joe the
Bootlegger" during Prohibition and the Ambassador to Great Britain under President Franklin D.
Roosevelt.

As Joe the Bootlegger, he would have booze sent to him from Scotland to the docks of New York which were controlled by the five Crime Syndicate families. But the U.S. Coast Guard was in on Joe Kennedy's racket too, because they would stamp the Scotch "medicine."

Once Kennedy got his "medicine" safely ashore, he would have Frank Costello distribute it to all those thirsty people in the "speakeasies" of an officially dry America. You may recall from an earlier chapter that I made a wisecrack to Frank Costello when I was a kid and we were visiting New York. Scotch was good to the Kennedys during Prohibition, and rumor has it that they still get a commission on every bottle of Scotch coming into the United States.

But it was a plain and simple fact that when Joe Kennedy wanted to make his son, Jack, President of the United States, he parlayed with the two people he knew who could make it happen: his old bootlegging partner Frank Costello, and Sam "the Cigar" Giancana, Boss of the Chicago Outfit.

Joe Kennedy said he included the Cigar in his deliberations to prove he had no affiliation with Frank Costello, but nobody in the know believed that for a New York second. Joe Kennedy earned his "Joe the Bootlegger" moniker from his active association with the Crime Syndicate during Prohibition, but he should have also been nicknamed "Hollywood Joe" for his starring role in the Outfit's movie business that was detailed in the preceding chapter.

Hollywood Joe Kennedy produced movies, lived large in sunny California, and while Rose was home in Massachusetts with the kids, he was squiring his mistress, Gloria Swanson, around Los Angeles. Joe Kennedy was involved with other starlets, but Gloria Swanson was his main squeeze.

The man who asked me to run for Alderman of the First Ward, Sam "the Cigar" Giancana, was my most reliable source for information about the Kennedy clan, and he described Jack Kennedy as a "warm-hearted, lovable playboy" who was completely unqualified to become the 35th President of the United States. Jack Kennedy and his siblings, Sam Giancana said, never worked a day in their lives. Sam Giancana first met Jack Kennedy right after he got elected to the U.S. Congress, and he said it was Joe Kennedy who put him there.

Jack Kennedy had the highest absentee record of any Congressman at the time, but he was always present for women who weren't his wife, particularly Angie Dickinson and Marilyn Monroe. You'd think that Marilyn was his favorite, but Kennedy always said that the "best piece of ass I ever had was Angie Dickinson."

And here's a true story of the Kennedy clan that you will enjoy: I was having dinner at Sages East, about five years after President Kennedy was assassinated, when in walked this big-shot car dealer and his gorgeous girlfriend. This guy sold all the Fords to the Chicago Police Department, so money was falling out of his pockets. He was a bachelor, but he was keeping his little honey in a luxurious Lake

Shore Drive apartment.

We got to talking, and, knowing that I was a politician, the young lady asked me if I had ever met John F. Kennedy.

"No, never," I said.

She smiled and proceeded to use Sam Giancana's exact words by describing Jack Kennedy exactly as a "warm-hearted, lovable guy."

Now, this young woman was a stewardess for United Airlines stationed in Washington, D.C., so I asked the obvious question. She said she first met Jack Kennedy after he was elected to Congress and he was on her "hop" from Boston to Washington.

In fairness, it should be noted he was a bachelor at the time. She caught the freshman Congressman's eye, and he started booking himself on flights that she worked. Soon they were having love affairs in New York and Boston.

"Well," I said, "when he became a United States Senator and he got married, did that end your love affair?"

"No," she said, "it never stopped. Then we'd go wherever he was going, and we would have a love affair there. Then he married Jackie (on September 12, 1953)."

"So when he got married and later became President of the United States, where could you go with him and not be recognized?"

"Simple," she said, "the Secret Service would come to my apartment, and they would bring men's clothing; shoes, socks, pants, jacket, usually a white shirt and tie, along with a trench coat and a fedora."

She would thus disguise herself as a man, and the Secret Service would drive her out to the airport where Air Force One was waiting far from any terminal. The President's plane was guarded around the clock, so this lady would pull up her collar and climb on board as though she were a Secret Service agent. No one was the wiser.

She would then sit in comfort for an hour or two, and then they would taxi the plane over to the terminal where a band would begin playing and the President would arrive and wave to all his loyal admirers.

President Kennedy would then hop on Air Force One and, before the plane had a chance to leave the ground, he would hop his favorite stewardess. All at the taxpayer's expense, mind you, and she said the last trip they took together was to Pittsburgh. It wasn't a long flight, but they made good use of their short time together, and it was the same drill when they arrived: an adoring crowd, the band playing, and a dapper young President off to make a speech to a labor union. But the President's mistress had to sit on the plane and wait, because it was surrounded by the Secret Service.

Kennedy finally finished making his speech in Pittsburgh glad-handing all the local politicians, and returned to the airport where they struck up the band again and the crowd waved and cheered.

"And," she said, "we were in bed again before the plane left the runway."

Do you think Jackie ever asked him what he really did on his trip to Pittsburgh? Who knows, but the lady I met at Sages East said she had to wait for more than two hours after they arrived back in Washington to leave the plane. When the crowds and press were gone, she put back on her disguise and had the Secret Service secretly return her to her apartment.

"So," I said at the end of her story, "did you like Jack?"

"Yes," she said without hesitation. "He was a fun, warm-hearted guy. I really miss him."

That, ladies and gentlemen, is a true story, even if I don't remember her name.

By the way, the only domestic trip Jackie Kennedy ever made with her husband was on November 22, 1963 to Dallas, Texas. We all remember how that trip ended, and we can all still picture her standing on Air Force One watching Lyndon B. Johnson being sworn in as President of the United States.

Jackie Kennedy certainly suffered, but she had suffered enough of Marilyn Monroe by May of 1962 when the blonde bombshell sang "Happy Birthday" to President Kennedy on national television.

Jacqueline Bouvier Kennedy gave JFK the following ultimatum: ditch Marilyn Monroe or divorce me. Kennedy compromised by passing Marilyn Monroe on to his little brother, Bobby. Keep it in the family, right?

The Kennedy brothers certainly shared a love of

blonde bombshells, but they had opposite person-
alities. While Jack was a "warm, fun-loving guy,"
brother Bobby was best described as "being arrogant and no fun at all." Bobby was dying to become
President himself, but then he fell for Marilyn
Monroe head over heels. And, as previously stated
in this book, it was Bobby Kennedy who made love
to Marilyn Monroe on the day she died of causes
that remain a mystery to everyone, but those who
are "in the know."

The world was certainly stunned when Marilyn
Monroe reportedly "died in her sleep" at her Brentwood, California home at the age of 36 on August
5, 1962. Marilyn Monroe, who was born Norma
Jeane Mortenson, had spent most of her childhood
in foster homes and orphanages and never knew
who her father was.

A truly tragic figure, she wed her 21-year-old
neighbor, Jimmy Dougherty, on June 19, 1942
when she was only 16 in order to keep from going
back to the orphanage. They were reported to be
happy together until he joined the Merchant Ma-
rines and was sent to the South Pacific in 1944.

After her husband went off to sea, she took a
job on the assembly line at the Radio Plane Muni-
tions factory in Burbank, California, and it was
while working there that she got her big break.

A photographer for Yank Magazine took one
look at that "photographer's dream" and decided to
include her in a photo story about women working
to support the war effort.

The camera loved her, and Norma Jeane was

modeling for popular magazines in no time.

She divorced Jimmy Dougherty in June of 1946, and signed her first studio contract, with Twentieth Century Fox, two months later. And then she ditched both her dark hair and her plain name by becoming the blonde bombshell the whole world knows as MARILYN MONROE.

Her career took off from there, and she went on to appear in 30 movies. Men everywhere wanted her, so little wonder that Joe Kennedy's sons would be any different. Yes, they both had their way with Marilyn Monroe, but they didn't exactly get away with it, did they? And they certainly do not emerge as white shining knights in this whole sorry story, do they?

Sam Giancana certainly was not a member of Bobby Kennedy's fan club. He told me that if that "ARROGANT PUNK EVER TRIED TO BECOME PRESIDENT, THEY'D KILL HIM JUST LIKE HIS BROTHER."

Sam didn't elaborate, but he certainly had no use for Bobby Kennedy and his enormous "I'm Bobby Kennedy" ego.

So while we'll probably never know the exact details of Marilyn Monroe's death, we do know that Bobby Kennedy had an argument with her just before she died. Marilyn said she had detailed the love affairs she had had with him and his brother in her diary. She was going to "leak" it to the press if he didn't satisfy her material demands.

I can say with assurance that nobody ever found that infamous diary. But they did discover various notes referring to the Kennedys, none of which were particularly detrimental to Jack and Bobby.

When Marilyn Monroe died in her home in the Los Angeles suburb of Brentwood on August 5, 1962, Bobby Kennedy covered his tracks by having someone drive him from Los Angeles to the San Francisco Airport. And guess what airline he flew back to Washington, D.C.? Bobby didn't fly any airline back to the capital, he went on a private plane owned by the Hotel and Restaurant Employees Union.

Commonly called the Bartenders Union, it was controlled totally by the Outfit. And you can bet that Bobby did not land at the main airport in D.C. No, he was landed at an outlying airport, met by the Secret Service, and whisked away so no one could question him about his activities that day.

How well did Bobby cover his tracks? Try to find any record of that plane taking off from San Francisco on August 5, 1962 and landing near Washington, D.C. the same day. Good luck.

I'll save you the trouble by telling you that the records were all expunged. Popular accounts of Marilyn Monroe's death say she died of an overdose of barbiturates. Though officially classified as a "probable suicide," the possibility of an accidental overdose has not been ruled out, while conspiracy theorists argue that she was murdered.

The official Marilyn Monroe website simply says she "died in her sleep." Theorize all you want, but I will tell you straight out that Marilyn Monroe was suffocated to death. And if indeed there was an autopsy, the results would have been doctored by the Kennedy brothers.

Marilyn Monroe never medicated herself with needles; she took her pills orally. So it would have been too difficult to stuff pills down her throat, especially with her housekeeper screaming in the background. They didn't want to leave any marks on her body, so they simply suffocated her to death.

We have focused so far on Jack Kennedy and his brother Bobby, but now we need to give their younger brother, Edward Moore "Ted" Kennedy, his due.

Ted Kennedy has been in office since November 1962 when he took his older brother Jack's seat in the United States Senate. And it was while running in the Massachusetts primary for that seat that Ted Kennedy was famously told by his opponent: "If your name was Edward Moore, instead of Edward Moore Kennedy, you wouldn't be standing here on this platform."

I am truly sorry that Senator Kennedy did not recover from cancer of the brain.. But I simply cannot sing the praises of a "media darling" who has never worked a minute in his life.

Like his two older brothers, he was a major womanizer. This despite his having once been married to a very attractive Joan Kennedy, who I used to see in Vail, Colorado where I had a home.

Funny, I would see Joan Kennedy in church with the children, but not with Senator Kennedy.

However, I did see Ted Kennedy himself and Senator John Tunney from California in the early 1960s while I was skiing at Aspen. They were with two charming young ladies (that were not their wives) skiing every day and having dinner in public.

The press was there, but they gave him a pass. Like they did in 1969 when he had his little "Chappaquiddick incident" and left Mary Jo Kopechne to drown in Poucha Pond after he had driven a car off the bridge. She had been one of his brother Bobby's "Boiler Room Girls," and he was driving her home after a party on Chappaquiddick Island. I'll save you the trouble of looking it up on the Internet by quoting Wikipedia's entry on Ted Kennedy which states that "Kennedy left the scene and did not call authorities until after Kopechne's body was discovered the following day."

On July 25, Kennedy pleaded guilty to leaving the scene of an accident and was given a sentence of two months in jail, suspended. That night, Kennedy gave a national broadcast in which he said, 'I regard as indefensible the fact that I did not report the accident to the police immediately,' but denied driving under the influence of alcohol and denied any immoral conduct between him and Kopechne.

"Kennedy asked the Massachusetts electorate whether he should stay in office, and after getting a favorable response, he did by getting 62 percent of the vote against an under-funded Republican in 1970 when he easily won re-election to the Senate." And, Wikipedia noted, "A grand jury on

Martha's Vineyard staged a two-day investigation in April 1970 but issued no indictment."

Ted Kennedy was completely exonerated for the death of 28-year-old Mary Jo Kopechne.

Did Kennedy money and power play a part?

You be the judge, but I will pass my own judgment on Joe the Bootlegger and his boys - they had no respect for anybody.

And the Kennedys really had it in for FBI Director J. Edgar Hoover. Bobby, as Attorney General, would have loved to have fired Hoover, but Hoover had files full of incriminating evidence against the Kennedys and their illegal and illicit activities. So Attorney General Robert Kennedy could bellyache all he wanted about how "bad J. Edgar Hoover is," but he couldn't touch him. No President could, because Hoover kept files on everybody.

And I can say for sure that one of Hoover's files contained this little Kennedy tidbit:

Jack Kennedy was married before he married Jacqueline Bouvier.

The records of Kennedy's first marriage had been expunged, but that crafty J. Edgar Hoover had managed to find one and keep it on file. What this meant, of course, was that having first been married in the Catholic Church, Jack Kennedy should not have been allowed to marry there a second time, to Jacqueline Bouvier. But the Kennedys do seem to get their way with the Catholic Church, don't they?

And that begs another church question: why did

the church sanction Jackie Kennedy's re-marriage to Greek shipping magnate, Aristotle Onassis?

Cardinal Spellman of New York provided the answer when he said: "Well, it's okay. She talked to me about it."

Do you think Cardinal Spellman would have given the same answer to some regular Bob or Betty from the back pew who wanted permission for a second marriage? I don't think so, and I really don't see any difference between these Kennedy people and Al Capone. In fact, I think the government people are the worst.

Like I told the news media in Chicago one time: "When I'm watching a government inquiry with known gangsters in front of them, I can't decide which side of the table the good guys are on. The bad guys are on both sides of the table."

And I'll tell you this: that when the government tells me I have to do something, I'd better do it or give up my freedom. On the other hand, I have never seen the Crime Syndicate put a gun to someone's head and order them to drink or gamble. Sure, they would put a gun to your head if you gambled with them and didn't pay when you lost. What business doesn't collect its debts?

But on the great scale of morality, I would have to give the Crime Syndicate a much higher grade than the government, despite what you read about them in our "unbiased" news media.

I maintain throughout this book that the Outfit was far more moral than our "trusted servants" in government, like the Kennedys, and I stand on that, because it is true. Just as it was true, as I said before, that the Outfit also owned the Movie Projectors Union in Chicago and thus controlled whose picture made it to the silver screen.

The Outfit controlled production in Hollywood through ownership of the Movie Union, but if some rogue outfit managed to start making a movie, they could put the kibosh on it by calling a strike before shooting was finished. Then, as I explained in the last chapter, Mr. Hot-Shot Producer would have to grease the right palms to get his movie in the can. And "Joe the Ambassador" Kennedy had been a big part of that racket when he was still known as "Joe the Bootlegger."

And while I'm popping the bubbles of popular fantasies, I want to put the needle to Chicago's very own Colonel Robert R. McCormick who boldly proclaimed his Chicago Tribune to be "the World's Greatest Newspaper."

Well, guess who the good Colonel turned to when Tribune workers went on strike?

Yes, Al Capone.

And when Capone had broken the strike and come for a chat with the Colonel, McCormick said to him: "You know, Al, I still have to write you up. You're the biggest news in Chicago."

And Capone answered: "That's all right with me, Colonel, but leave my family alone."

Colonel McCormick agreed, and he kept his promise. Now let's motor over to the Motor City and look at Detroit's legendary Henry Ford who broke up a strike against his Ford Motor Company with a little help from the heavies of the notorious Purple Gang.

Was Henry Ford any better than Al Capone? You tell me.

And then we had Cornelius Vanderbilt who built his railroad empire on the backs of Italian immigrants who had been passed through Ellis Island with no paperwork. They were completely expendable, because nobody knew who they were.

Vanderbilt just knew that their blood, sweat and tears were good for making him one of America's first billionaires. And the great American entrepreneur they called "the Commodore," would be pleased to see they are using his same system of exploitation of helpless immigrants on our southern border today.

Likes attract, so Commodore Vanderbilt got with oil baron John D. Rockefeller and agreed that the only oil that would be shipped on Vanderbilt's railroads would be "black gold" from Rockefeller's Standard Oil Company.

Rockefeller, so you know, waged a little oil war in Colorado in which more than 120 people were killed. He wanted control, and he got it, no matter who stood in his way. So when the other drillers tried to get their oil to the markets in the east, they found that Vanderbilt didn't have any trains available. And if Rockefeller's competitors ever did find a way to move their oil, they had to pay so much that they were consistently undersold at the pump by Standard Oil.

There were no trucks in those days, so if you

wanted to move your oil from the fields in Pennsylvania to Illinois, then you needed rail, and Cornelius Vanderbilt had the monopoly there. But we don't think of the 19th Century's Commodore Vanderbilt and John D. Rockefeller as gangsters, do we? No, they are regarded as pillars of American capitalism.

How about that 20th Century fox, Howard Hughes? Although the history books describe him as a daring American aviator, industrialist, and wealthy philanthropist, Howard Hughes was best known to certain people for his willingness to play ball with the Crime Syndicate.

Hughes gladly turned to the Outfit when he wanted to prevent his workers from striking. So the Outfit "crafted" a union deal for our famous flyboy that prohibited workers from striking while Hughes' company was filling government contracts. And his company always seemed to be filling government contracts.

The Outfit helped Howard Hughes overcome his labor problems, and he returned the favor when the feds put the heat on Las Vegas and drove the various Crime Syndicates out of the casinos there. That meant that the Chicago Outfit had to give up the Stardust, and the Purple Gang of Detroit had to step away from the Aladdin.

Ditto for the Cleveland Mob with their Desert Inn and the New York Mob with the Tropicana. They all had to keep their hands off with the feds breathing down their necks, so who better to step in and represent their interests than foursquare

Howard Hughes? He had the money and the moxie to buy all those casinos, and he was more than happy to let the various Syndicates serve as shadow partners.

Yul Brynner was another famous figure who was willing to play ball with the Outfit. You may recall that the Russian-born actor's breakthrough role was the lead in The King and I. Well, guess who got him the part?

Sam Giancana himself, and he got a Yorkshire Terrier as a gift from a grateful Yul Brynner who went on to appear in The Ten Commandments and co-star in The Magnificent Seven. And let us not forget our aforementioned singer from Hoboken, New Jersey, Frank Sinatra.

Frank's career was heading south in a hurry, and he knew he needed to get a major part in the 1953 classic, "From Here to Eternity" with Burt Lancaster and Debra Kerr. So he went to the real Godfather, Sam Giancana. And begged the Cigar to talk to the producer on his behalf.

The Cigar made the call and said: "If you want to make the movie, then he's the guy who is going to star in that role."

And, off the record, he probably added: "We're in a position to give you bigger bookings and more dates."

Frank Sinatra also found his singing career drifting away from him when he couldn't get out of a long-term contract with bandleader Tommy Dorsey. Sinatra still had his pipes, but he didn't have his clout, so he went to Giancana for help, and suddenly Tommy Dorsey is all for releasing Frank Sinatra from his contract.

I don't think they threatened Tommy; I think they just lined his pockets with new contracts.

Nobody at that time dreamed Frank Sinatra would become the super star that we know him as. They thought he was too big for his britches. Everybody was against him, because Frank had turned on those who had done him favors. So he could just go off on his own and flop, and that would be the end of him. Good riddance to that bum from Hoboken.

Frank Sinatra certainly did struggle on his own, and for four or five years he sang on a local radio show for only $50 a week. But he was winning fans, and one of them was Sam Giancana who was becoming the boss of the Chicago Outfit.

The Cigar always said: "I love this guy Sinatra."

I don't know why, but he did.

When I was about 20, I drove my older brother to his army duty at Fort Bliss and then kept his I.D. and the new car my dad had given him. So a friend and I used that to our advantage by taking a road trip out west.

When we got to Las Vegas, we found that Frank Sinatra was appearing at the Desert Inn. This was his big break, because he had never been allowed to appear on "the Strip" before 1951. So my friend and I found ourselves standing in the casino when this waitress comes along and says: "Why don't you two guys come in and see Frank Sinatra?"

We knew who he was, so we did. The drinks were 65 cents, and the place was two-thirds empty, but Sinatra put on a terrific show. I had always thought Sinatra was a great, great singer, and he didn't disappoint us that night. And what made that night even more memorable was that we got to see Sinatra's girlfriend of the moment, Ava Gardner, and movie star Rory Calhoun.

We found ourselves sitting near them, and so one of the people Rory Calhoun was with, said to him: "I'd like meet Ava Gardner."

So Rory calls, one star to another, "Ava, Ava!"

And Ava says: "Oh, Rory, how are you?"

Rory says fine and tells Ava he wants to introduce her to Mr. and Mrs. So-and-So. Ava Gardener graciously introduces herself to the couple with a fine "how do you do?"

And Mr. So-and-So says: "I've always been a great fan of yours."

You are probably wondering about me and my friend. Why didn't we go over and get ourselves introduced to Ava Gardner and Rory Calhoun.

I was 20 at the time, all right?

But I will tell you that we enjoyed Frank Sinatra's entire show and feasted our eyes on Ava Gardner when she walked out after it was over. She was a knockout all right, but, frankly, I have seen better bodies.

Donnie Parrillo

CHAPTER THIRTEEN

THE FBI
(HOOVER AT THE HELM)

Think FBI, and you naturally think J. Edgar Hoover, because he was not only the bureau's first director, but he was at the helm when most of the events described in this book were unfolding.

Many people maligned J. Edgar Hoover, but believe me, he was a very effective and efficient Director of the Federal Bureau of Investigation. Hoover was appointed director of the Bureau of Investigation - predecessor to the FBI - in 1924, and he helped found the FBI in 1935 and remained director until his death in 1972.

You have to credit Hoover for building the FBI into the powerful crime-fighting agency that it is now.

But Hoover still gets a bum rap for chasing communists instead of fighting organized crime.

In Hoover's defense, I have to say that he DID

pursue organized crime once he was given the legal backing he needed in the 1940s. Hoover had to work with the laws that were on the books, and bank robbery was not a federal offense unless the robbers crossed state lines with their loot.

So in the beginning, FBI agents could only investigate federal crimes. So in Chicago they would have to ask the local police to make the arrest after they caught a bootlegger.

J. Edgar Hoover once said that there is no such thing as the Mafia in the United States, and he was absolutely right. There never was and never will be one organized syndicate governing all the rackets in this country.

The Mafia, according to an article provided by the Italian Consulate in Chicago titled "The True Story of the Mafia A Lost Family of Honor," was actually a secret society that arose in 1282 to defeat the French Angevins who "held a tight grip on Sicily."

The secret society's battle cry was: "morte alla Francia Italia anelia." That is Italian for: "death to the French is Italy's cry."

Take the first letters of the English translation of that 13th century battle cry, and you have M-A-F-I-A as in Mafia. The word Mafia was first published in 1862 in a play by Giuseppe Rizzuto called I Mafiosi della Vicaria (The Mafia in the Vicarage) about a secret criminal group in the prisons of Palermo.

In Sicily, according to the Italian government, the word mafia means "manly," and is often applied to someone without necessarily meaning they were a criminal.

Sicily, of course, had to adapt to numerous foreign invasions: Arabs in the 9th century, Normans in the 11th century, the aforementioned French in the 12th, Spanish in the 15th, as well as invasions by the Germans, Austrians, and Greeks.

So secret societies were needed in Sicily to resist these foreign invaders and rulers. These societies were formed not only to defeat the French rulers but to protect and feed Italian families in Palermo and surrounding areas. Since most of the villagers were related, each family picked a member to head their family, and they called them "capodecina" or "capos" for short.

The capodecina would pick men from the village to take with him to the hills. And before the men left to fight the French, they would have to pledge their loyalty, support and omerta, or the code of silence.

The oath in English sounded like this: "I (name) want to enter into this secret organization to protect my family and to protect my brothers. Morte alla Francia Italia anelia! (Death to the French is Italy's cry!)" They would then cut the right index finger or hand and say: "With my blood and the blood of all the saints, and the souls of my children" (the sign of the cross is made) "I swear not to divulge this secret and to obey with love and omerta. I enter alive into this organization and leave it only in death."

The members of this secret society raided food

and supplies from the French and were brutally tortured and killed when caught. This society has survived through the centuries and is so secret that only members know other members.

What Americans call Mafia in this country is believed to have been started by Don Vito Cascio Ferro in 1893 after he fled to New York following the murder of banker Emanuele Notarbartolo in Sicily.

More society members fled to American during the 1920s when Mussolini attempted to eradicate the Mafia in Sicily. When the Allies liberated Italy during World War II, they freed anti-Mussolini prisoners, including many society members. Some were installed in positions of power and thus began to interweave politics and organized crime in Italy. The society moved from the rural hills to the cities of Sicily.

The Sicilians have also developed co-operative agreements with other secret Italian societies, the Camorra and Ndrangheta, but remain the controlling organization.

The Sicilians, according to the article from the Italian government, are flexible and can work with many nationalities. "The major threat to the Sicilians and the society is their own periodic bloodletting feuds. If the society that was called Mafia in the 12th century was alive and well today; there would not be a need for government programs. All would prosper. Italians need to look close at their families and friends."

So, concludes the article, "there is no Mafia; it

does not exist anymore, but there is a chance for Italians to work together with their families and friends to make life better and more prosperous."

J. Edgar Hoover, as you can see, was not alone in saying there is no such thing as the Mafia. It doesn't exist in Italy, as the Italian government just said, and, like Hoover said so long ago, it doesn't exist in the United States.

It was impossible in Hoover's day, and it is impossible now, even with the Internet and what have you.

As I have already explained, crime organizations were divided by cities, with some families running New York and others controlling Cleveland, Chicago, St. Louis, and Kansas City. There was never an organized control of either Florida or Los Angeles, and Las Vegas was considered an open city. These various gangs would help one another when called to do so, but they were never dominated or controlled by any one person. These crime syndicates were started by poor people looking to get ahead in America, and they started with bootlegging when the government gave them the "gift" of Prohibition. When Prohibition was repealed, they turned to the next promising racket like bookmaking. And it wasn't as if they were sent here to begin lives of organized crime. So Hoover was absolutely right when he said there is no such thing as the Mafia in the United States, because there is not. And it is worth repeating that Bobby Kennedy absolutely detested J. Edgar Hoover.

As Attorney General, Kennedy could have fired

Hoover any time he wanted, but he declined to do so, because, as I have said, Hoover had the goods on the dirty dealings of the Kennedy family. All on file and ready to be released anytime Bobby Kennedy got a little too full of himself.

Not only did Hoover have files on Bobby and Jack Kennedy's trysts with Marilyn Monroe, he had documented "Joe the Bootlegger" Kennedy's links to crime syndicates in New York and around the country.

Hoover's FBI also set their sights on First Ward headquarters in Chicago and had tapped all of their telephone lines.

Shortly after Lyndon Johnson became President, he ordered all the tapping of telephone lines and bugging removed. But I can tell you that the instrument was never removed, and I know this from Bill Roemer, who was the FBI agent in charge of investigating organized crime in Chicago for 25 years. The monitoring equipment is still in the molding and light sockets of the 100 North La-Salle building which once housed the First Ward headquarters.

Hoover knew about President John F. Kennedy's extramarital activities because he had had Sam Giancana's phone tapped. He thus learned that the Outfit Boss and the President of the United States were screwing the same girl, Judith Wexner.

Hoover, whose own sexual proclivities are the subject of a separate book, gladly took the tapes to the White House and played them for President Kennedy. You can imagine Kennedy's reaction, and when he calmed down, he prevailed upon Hoover to destroy the tapes.

Who knows what Hoover did with those incriminating tapes, but they have yet to resurface. Someone close to Hoover, however, did leak the records of the calls between that girl in California and Giancana and the White House.

As a matter of fact, that girl was at Giancana's house in Oak Park one time when she picked up his phone and called President Kennedy on his direct line, and he answered. The FBI got that call on tape too.

The FBI was highly efficient, considering all the restraints placed on them by the law. They were zealous too, and so when Hoover ordered an end to the bugging of homes and offices, quite a few agents continued to do so. Hoover's main beef was that "we could not use it in court," but he knew perfectly well that all that illegal taping was providing some excellent intelligence on the FBI's quarry. Hoover insisted that his agents never frame anyone, and that they won their convictions with legally obtained evidence.

Now to William Roemer and his various books about organized crime. He meant well, I am sure, but I have to tell you that his books were misleading at best and erroneous at worst. Don't get me wrong: Roemer was a sincere and honest person, and he was a Notre Dame graduate and had gone to law school.

But poor Bill Roemer was a duck out of water trying to find out about organized crime. For example, he never won a single conviction during his 25 years as head of the FBI's Organized Crime Bureau. That's not the kind of record needed to write so-called authoritative books about organized crime. But that's one man's opinion.

I met Bill Roemer at the Kroch's & Brentano's Bookstore on Michigan Avenue where he was signing copies of his latest book on organized crime. My ex-wife asked me to get an autographed copy, so I gladly got in line. And when I started toward the star author, Roemer thanked me for coming to his book signing party. He didn't know me, and I didn't know him. So I said, "Well, my ex-wife says she's a friend of yours. She's the one who told me to come here to get the book. Could you autograph it to her?"

"Sure," he said, "what's her name?"

"Nancy Reilly."

Roemer stopped writing and looked up at me. "Are you the Alderman?"

"Yes, I am."

"You know, I always wanted to meet you," he said.

"Bill," I said, "I always wanted to meet you too, but not in the 1960s. I wanted to meet you in the 1990s."

We hit it off that day, and I think we could have become good friends if we had had the chance.

And there seemed to be a chance about a year after the book signing when my daughter, who lives in Arizona, and I drove down to Tucson to have a luncheon meeting with Bill Roemer.

We agreed over lunch that we would write a book together, like Muhammad Ali and Howard Cosell - the good guy and the bad guy. So, I started to tell Bill Roemer about some of the discrepancies I had found in his book. Now, you have to picture the setting: a restaurant that seated 70 to 80 people.

I said to him, "In your book, you say that Joey Aiuppa, who was the boss of Cicero for over 40 years, had to go to Giancana and tell him that he was broke, and that he needed more territory." I paused, pointed around that big restaurant and added, "Bill, Joey Aiuppa could fill up this restaurant with hundred dollar bills from floor to ceiling, and he wouldn't even know they were gone. He was the boss of the second most lucrative crime group in Chicago for 40 years. He had to have made millions of dollars practically every year. He didn't need to go to Giancana for more territory."

And then I tactfully pointed out another glaring discrepancy: Roemer's assertion that Tony Spilatro was the one who had given Sam Giancana his dose of Taylor Street Justice while he was making sausage in his basement in Oak Park.

I reminded him that Spilatro was made a boss in Las Vegas by the Chicago Outfit, overseeing all the casinos there. Unfortunately, he got his hand caught in the till, and he was brought back to Chicago and beaten to death with his brother and buried in an Indiana cornfield.

I told Bill Roemer, "Spilatro was not the one who killed Giancana."

"Well," he asked, "who did?"

"His bodyguard."

I decline to reveal his name out of respect to his family who still live in the Chicago area. Roemer also recalled a confrontation that would be featured in the A&E television network's movie about Sam Giancana's relationship with Phyllis McGuire called "Sugar Time."

The film depicted that time at O'Hare Field when Roemer and some other FBI agents met Sam Giancana and Phyllis McGuire as they got off the plane and got into a nasty verbal confrontation with them. Foul language flew in both directions.

The film ended by vindicating me and proving Bill Roemer and the FBI wrong.

Roemer admitted to me at that Tucson restaurant that he had a strong personal dislike for Giancana and that the angry words at O'Hare really had been said.

So I told him, "It's because you're not Italian. You don't understand our way of life. If you'd go up and talk to him like a gentleman, he'd have answered you like a gentleman."

I like to think that I got through to Bill Roemer that day in Tucson, because when A&E broadcast "Sugar Time" about a month later, they identified Giancana's killer as his bodyguard, not Tony Spilatro.

And since my meeting with Bill Roemer, the entire FBI has known who gave Sam Giancana Taylor Street Justice. But do they know who ordered the hit? Believe me, there were all kinds of rumors flying about what was going to happen to Sam Giancana when he came back from his nine-year "exile" in Mexico.

You may recall from earlier in the book that the Cigar had flown to Mexico after serving a year in Cook County Jail for refusing to testify before a Federal Grand Jury. Word on the street had it that when Sam Giancana got settled back in Chicago he was going to retake control of the Outfit and demand a bigger share for himself. Other rumors had him becoming a government witness, which I would absolutely swear he would never do.

So Bill Roemer asked me over lunch how I knew Sam Giancana so well. "He used to drive me and my brother to school occasionally, and my father was his lawyer."

My turn, so I asked Bill Roemer if he had ever tapped my phone or opened my mail. Roemer confessed that he had assigned FBI agents to my "account."

The problem, he said, was that I had become a millionaire the old-fashioned way: I had worked for it as a legitimate businessman. The FBI could not pin anything on me, because there was nothing to pin on me. I was a legitimate businessman, and all the money I earned as Alderman of the First Ward was made legitimately through the enhancement of bank deposits for me and through real estate connections.

Roemer was also amazed at how much I knew about organized crime. In fact, he had been quoted as saying that "nobody in America understands the relationship between organized crime and politics and legitimate business better than Don Parrillo."

So I explained to Bill Roemer that when you're born and raised in the old Taylor Street neighborhood and your father is an attorney and a political bigwig, you're kind of into it before you even know what it is, or what it's all about.

"You want to find out more about organized crime," I told Roemer, "then go hang around Taylor Street, the old neighborhood. You'll know more in two hours down there than you'll know in two years sitting in your office downtown."

Sadly, Bill Roemer and I never got to write our good guy/bad guy book, because he was diagnosed with lung cancer about seven months after our meeting. He had never touched tobacco or liquor and worked out all the time, but he got lung cancer just the same, and it took him down like everybody else.

I miss him still, and I still think we would have become great friends, had he lived. As he was dying, I would call him and say, "When are we going to get together on the book, Bill?"

And he would say, "Well, give me another few weeks until I get my strength back."

But we both knew that was never going to happen, because he was dying.

Rest in peace, Bill Roemer, and maybe we'll finally get to write that book when we meet in heaven.

The FBI and other law enforcement agencies are very good at capturing criminals, but what they often lack is a knowledge of whom ordered the crime in the first place and why they ordered it. What was the benefit? What did the victim do to deserve "Taylor Street Justice?"

You had to have done something wrong to deserve such justice, and law enforcement officials are often unable to connect the dots. But they keep trying, and so do a group of very well-educated people in Chicago who call themselves the "Merry Gangster Society."

I have been on bus tours with these high-society types as we passed gangsters' big homes in Oak Park and River Forest. Sure enough, there was my mother's house along the tour, because she had moved to River Forest from the old neighborhood. But those Merry Gangster types know they can believe me when they call for information about this or that crime figure.

It's all in my head, so I just give them names, dates, and entire biographies without having to look anything up. They want to know the date somebody got Taylor Street Justice, I have it in my head. It's all a part of me, because I grew up in that environment.

So one day the head of the Merry Gangster Society asked me to join them on a bus tour, and they promised that I did not have to reveal my true identity. My son and I would be just another pair of organized-crime buffs aboard that open-air bus.

I had a hard time holding my tongue, especially when we went right past the house I grew up in. And I was surprised to see that most of those

40-some people on the bus were well-educated, middle-aged women. They were fascinated by organized crime, and never stopped asking questions of the guide. So I really had to hold my breath when one of them asked, "Is it really true that the First Ward of Chicago made John F. Kennedy President of the United States?"

I tapped my son and said, "I hope the heck the guide doesn't tell them that the Alderman of the First Ward is sitting right here on the bus."

The guide probably should have called on me, because he not only denied that the First Ward put Kennedy in the White House in 1960, but he gave the wrong vote totals.

And he didn't realize that the First Ward had controlled 11 other wards, the so-called River Wards. Those are the wards, you may recall, in which you didn't count the votes, you weighed them.

But those Merry Gangster Society people on the bus just lapped it up, because organized crime is the most fascinating subject you can delve into. Witness the never-ending stream of movies, TV shows, and books about organized crime. Taylor Street Justice is pure gold for any enterprising producer or publisher.

But isn't it ironic that the subject of all those popular movies and books began to decline in the 1970s. Yes, that was the beginning of the end of what we know as "Organized Crime in America."

The bosses of the various syndicates knew the clock was winding down, but not because of pressure from the FBI or other law enforcement agencies. They knew the end was in sight when two ominous laws were enacted.

First, there was the Immunity Law, which allowed the Chief Judge of of the Circuit to incarcerate you for refusing to testify before the Grand Jury. And, as we saw with Sam Giancana, you were incarcerated for the full term of the Grand Jury. In his case, it was a full year in Cook County Jail.

Ironically, the Immunity Law's first victim was its author, Nixon's Attorney General, John Mitchell.

But the second law was more devastating than the first, because it created the highly successful Witness Protection Program. Meaning that before a witness agreed to tell his story, the government had to promise him protection and give him a new identity and home.

Organized crime only caught one such witness, and it was because the guy had made a stupid mistake.

The Witness Protection Program had moved him to Phoenix, Arizona, and everything was fine until he got in an automobile accident and stupidly filed a lawsuit under his real name. A syndicate snitch caught that and made a call that resulted in some Taylor Street Justice in sunny Arizona just three days later.

He was the only one the syndicates have been able to reach, so the Witness Protection Program has proved to be a potent tool in the government's war on organized crime.

People think that the old-time gangsters were more loyal and honorable than their later associates. Not true. In the old days there was no Immunity Law or Witness Protection Program - just Taylor Street Justice.

You squealed, you got Taylor Street Justice.

So credit those two laws with bringing down organized crime in America.

But I do not want to end this chapter without saluting the FBI and saying that most of the agents I have met have been first-class, educated people.

America is fortunate to have a Federal Bureau of Investigation on duty 24/7. There are more than enough white-collar criminals and terrorists for them to pursue, and, as J. Edgar Hoover said, "They always get their man."

I am fortunate to have met Bill Roemer, especially since I met him in the 1990s, not the 1960s. Somebody else like him will probably write a book or two about organized crime, but they won't be factual either.

If you want to know the real facts, call me. I'll tell you.

As I once said to the FBI's Bill Roemer, "Bill, I probably have forgotten more about organized crime than you will ever know."

CHAPTER FOURTEEN

CAL-NEVA LODGE
(A FUN WEEKEND)

Sam Giancana told me this story after his falling-out with the Kennedys, and FBI agent Bill Roemer later verified it.

Sam began and ended his incredible but true tale by saying, "You see, Donnie, this only proves that any jack-off is liable to become President of the United States."

That got your attention, didn't it? And well it should, because Giancana was speaking to me of a truly epic weekend in the fall of 1961 that he spent with some very colorful people at the Cal-Neva Lodge in beautiful Lake Tahoe, Nevada.

Come along with me now as I take you back to that lodge that straddled the California/Nevada line and look in on the Cigar and his associates who were gathered not for any business purpose but strictly for "fun and sex."

Who were the players?

Well, I have already listed "the Cigar" from Chicago, and I must add that little, skinny singer from Hoboken, New Jersey who later double-crossed the Cigar. Marilyn Monroe, who was the leading star of the time, was there as well as one other girl that the FBI was not able to identify. Her name was Jeanie Carmen, and I later learned that she died in Scottsdale, Arizona in 2007.

And, yes, the FBI was there thanks to an illegal wiretap they had placed on Sam Giancana's phone. So they knew all about this fun little weekend at the Cal-Neva Lodge that the Cigar and his associates were planning.

But pity the poor FBI because they did not have sufficient time in which to obtain a warrant for a legal wiretap of the lodge. So, being good gum-shoes, they found out what room the Cigar and company were going to use and they illegally bugged it and wiretapped the phones.

Resourceful guys, those FBI agents. J. Edgar Hoover, as I said in the last chapter, frowned on obtaining information in this manner, but he knew it would lead to legitimate evidence that could be used in court.

Now to the Cal-Neva Lodge itself which was owned partly by the Cigar, partly by that skinny singer from Hoboken, Frank Sinatra, and partly by other partners. By today's standards, the Cal-Neva would look like a third-rate motel. But it was quite the palace in its day, and the owners had been clever enough to have had 99.9 percent of it built on the

Nevada side of the line where gambling was legal. That little smidgen in California was literally for window dressing.

They also got the advantage of having almost all of their building in Nevada where taxes were substantially lower. To amuse and educate their guests, they had a white line drawn through the middle of the sitting room to show them what state they were in.

And what a state the Cigar and his friends must have been in that afternoon when they arrived for a long weekend of sex, wine, and song. And those FBI agents must have been hopped-up too because they had things so well bugged that they were even going to be able to listen in on all that hot sex with the likes of Marilyn Monroe herself.

The FBI heard more of Marilyn than they bargained for that weekend, because they got her on tape going at it with that other girl. Oh, yes!

But even stranger than that was the unexpected call they intercepted when Marilyn Monroe dialed a very private number and was greeted by none other than President John F. Kennedy. You younger and more sensitive readers might want to skip ahead a few paragraphs, because what I am about to tell you is for adults only. Marilyn Monroe and the President of the United States of America, the leader of the Free World, had phone sex for a good ten minutes.

They blistered the ears of those FBI snoopers with their explicit language, and can you imagine the President of the United States whacking his yoyo on the telephone? Marilyn Monroe certainly could.

Better yet, imagine what Marilyn Monroe was doing while she was talking dirty to President Kennedy.

The tape of that long-distance lovemaking was made illegally, so it was never used in court. But the FBI agents never destroyed the tape either. They brought it back to their offices in California, and when other agents would visit, they would play the tape over and over again and laugh like hell.

And they would later capture Bobby Kennedy on tape with Marilyn Monroe having phone sex with her. I tell you, those Kennedy brothers were way ahead of their time. As for Marilyn Monroe, the Cigar always maintained she was Bobby's heart-throb, not Jack's.

As previously stated, John F. Kennedy's favorite piece of ass was Angie Dickinson. He would, in fact, describe her as the best piece of ass he ever had.

My sources for all this were impeccable: Sam "the Cigar" Giancana and the FBI's Bill Roemer from the previous chapter. This sex-capade took place at one of the last times that the Kennedys, Frank Sinatra, and the Cigar were still friends. To borrow a phrase from the Kennedy PR machine, it was the golden age of Camelot.

They were all in good spirits and, as the week-end progressed, they told that other girl, Jeanie or Joanie, that when she played blackjack in the casino she would win $10,000, guaranteed. Her win was guaranteed because her assigned dealer was a "mechanic" who could deal her whatever card she needed to win. And she won her $10,000.

I stayed at the Cal-Neva Lodge in 1990 and found that they have two notable rooms for rent: the Marilyn Monroe Room, and the Frank Sinatra Room.

Well, being a red-blooded American male, I chose the former so I can always say that I slept in the same bed with Marilyn Monroe.

Unfortunately, she wasn't there at the time, and the room was so dingy, I found it almost impossible to believe that the star had ever stayed there. My room was barely big enough for a bed and a dresser, and the bathroom was almost too small to use properly.

And they were telling us guests that there were passageways under the lodge that enabled the stars to go from their rooms to the stage without being seen by the public, but I was not inclined to believe that after a good look at the place.

And that fall weekend of wine, women, and song was really the last hurrah for the Cal-Neva Lodge, because the Nevada Gaming Commission lowered the boom on the owners after the national press picked up the sex-capade story.

The commission forced Frank Sinatra and Sam Giancana, who was listed under an assumed name, to sell their shares of the lodge.

So 1961 was really a bad year for the Cal-Neva Lodge, and it fractured the once chummy relationship between Frank Sinatra and the Kennedys.

It was in April of 1961 that Kennedy's "carefully planned" invasion of Cuba had ended in total disaster at the Bay of Pigs. You have already read about the consequences for the Kennedys of their failure to reclaim Cuba for the Cigar and company.

And, as I said, you can draw a straight line from the Bay of Pigs disaster in April 1961 to the dark events in Dallas on November 22, 1963.

But 1961 brought even worse news to the Kennedy clan with the incapacitation of the patriarch, "Joe the Bootlegger" Kennedy. The old man suffered a debilitating stroke that year, and he would remain mentally impaired until his death in November 1969.

Joe the Ambassador was no longer in a position to tell his son how to run the country. He simply disappeared from sight and was not heard from again until his death, and then he was just a footnote to history.

As I have said, the Cigar was very unhappy that the Bay of Pigs invasion failed. Crime syndicate money and muscle had put Kennedy in the White House with the explicit understanding that he would put Cuba back in their hands, and so the other crime bosses came down hard on the Cigar after the Bay of Pigs fiasco. They pressured him to pressure President Kennedy to try again to get Cuba back.

But the Cigar's timing couldn't have been worse, because with Joe the Bootlegger suddenly sidelined by a stroke, his boys were starting to shy away from the racketeers with whom he had done so much business in the past.

Bobby Kennedy, as Attorney General, had promised to keep his hands off the crime syndicates, but suddenly he was on the attack. The other bosses appealed frantically to the Cigar for relief. He could have called off Bobby had old Joe the Bootlegger still been in control of his faculties, but his stroke had taken him out of the game.

So Bobby, with his big brother cheering him on, got tough on organized crime and literally bit the hands that had fed his family for so many profitable years.

As I said earlier in this book, "People who are born with the silver spoon in their mouths never appreciate what you do for them. They assume they have it coming to them."

So long as old Joe Kennedy was alive and alert, his sons would have to leave his racketeering associates alone. That's because the FBI, and the crime syndicates both had the goods on Joe Kennedy.

Bobby Kennedy turned up the heat about eight months after his father suffered his stroke, and he first went after the people who had generously contributed to his brother's campaign.

The Cigar went to Frank Sinatra and said, "Would you go to the President and tell him to tell his brother to call off these investigation?"

They had all been friends, so why not?

But Frank Sinatra hesitated, and that really burned up the Cigar. So he told Sinatra to go back to Bobby Kennedy and make it perfectly clear that the target of his indictment was a close personal friend of Giancana's.

No can do, says Frank Sinatra. "I can't let the Kennedys know you could tell me what to do. It would kill off my relationship with them."

You may recall from earlier in the book that Sinatra pulled this same stunt in New York City when he was a young singer trying to get out of a long-term contract with bandleader Tommy Dorsey. The crime syndicate in New York had intervened for Sinatra. They simply greased Dorsey's palm, and he released Sinatra from the contract, freeing him to pursue his solo career.

Sinatra, of course, became a big star, but did he express his gratitude to the crime syndicate in New York? No, he figured he was too big to thank them.

So all the syndicates in America turned their backs on him, and you could say that while he never lost his voice, he certainly lost his image.

When members of the Chicago Outfit got hit with subpoenas in the middle of 1962, they naturally wondered what happened to their "clout" with the President and his Attorney General.

So the Cigar went back to Sinatra and told him, "Go tell Bobby Kennedy to leave our people alone. That was part of our agreement with him."

Once again, Sinatra refused to intercede on behalf of the man who had taken him from nowhere and put him on top of the world of entertainment. There is no doubt in my mind that if Giancana had not been forced to go to Mexico after he got out

of Cook County Jail that he would have had Frank
Sinatra killed.

And to add insult to injury, the Cigar later
learned that the Kennedys had told Sinatra that he
didn't need some Chicago gangster as a friend when
he had them. They told him to break with Giancana, and that really was the beginning of the end
of their relationship.

After Cal-Neva, Giancana's name was entered in
the black book of Las Vegas, meaning that the
Nevada Gaming Commission had made him perso-
na non grata in all gambling casinos in the state.
Their prohibition was so severe that Giancana
couldn't even go to Las Vegas to romance Phyllis
McGuire. So he would meet her at a ranch near Las
Vegas. But that was no fun, because he loved Las
Vegas and wanted to be there with her. And he
didn't like the weather in Florida, and Palm Springs
was off-limits because he had always stayed at
Frank Sinatra's house there.

So the sun set on the Cigar's happy life in the
limelight with the stars and celebrities. And those
same people who had enjoyed his company started
to shun him because they realized he no longer had
any clout with the Kennedy family.

He was no longer friends with singing sensation
Frank Sinatra, and they knew he was having his own
troubles with the Chicago crime syndicate, so they
gave him the cold shoulder.

But the Cigar adapted as best he could and
started leading a quieter life in and around Chicago. He would only leave town to be with Phyllis

McGuire, and he rarely dined at his favorite restaurant, the Armory Lounge. And the quieter and less obvious Sam Giancana became, the happier the Chicago Outfit was, because they did not share his love of the limelight.

But, as I detailed in the previous chapter, the limelight still found the Cigar, such as the time he and Phyllis McGuire were met at O'Hare by a group of FBI agents who provoked a screaming argument with them. The Chicago papers ate it up.

Then, of course, we had the assassination of President John F. Kennedy on November 22, 1963, and Sam Giancana was completely without any connection to the White House. He had no clout with Lyndon Johnson, and the other syndicates around the country were all over him wondering just what they had gotten in return for all the money and muscle they had invested in electing Jack Kennedy President of the United States.

Kennedy had appointed his brother, Bobby, Attorney General, and Bobby turned around and put more pressure on the syndicates than his predecessor had.

So when Sam Giancana was finally served with a subpoena, he knew his end was in sight. He served that year in Cook County Jail for refusing to testify before the Grand Jury, fled to Mexico for nine years, and then came back to hear his own requiem.

Yes, as you have already read, Sam "the Cigar" Giancana got his own dose of Taylor Street Justice while making sausage in the basement of his home in Oak Park on June 19, 1975.

But he never tired of talking about that amazing fall weekend at the Cal-Neva Lodge, and always finished the story with the words that began this chapter, "You see, Donnie, this only proves that any jack-off is liable to become President of the United States."

Donnie Parrillo

CHAPTER FIFTEEN

THE CIGAR IS EXTINGUISHED
(TAYLOR STREET JUSTICE)

June 19, 1975 found me driving north on the Tri-State Tollway to the North Shore to play in a "Hullabaloo" golf tournament at Bob-o-Link Country Club in Highland Park. I was listening to some good music on the radio when the announcer broke in with a news bulletin about Sam Giancana and a body at his house in Oak Park.

My first thought was who would be stupid enough to kill somebody and put the body near the Cigar's house?

I continued on my way thinking they must have made a big mistake. The music came back on, and all was well until they read the news at the top of the hour.

I nearly drove off the tollway, because they reported that the "bullet-riddled body of Sam Giancana had been found in the basement of his home in Oak Park, Illinois." Somebody, they said, had emptied a .22-caliber weapon into his neck and head. I was trembling so badly I had to pull over. The Cigar had reportedly been gunned down in his own basement.

Sam Giancana had been served with Taylor Street Justice.

I was too shocked to do anything but just sit there and try to breathe. All kinds of images of him flashed through my mind, and I particularly remembered television coverage of him getting off that plane from Mexico at O'Hare and walking through the terminal in his pajamas and a heavy growth of beard.

It was impossible to picture him falling that far, and, unbelievably, they were reporting that he had been murdered in his own basement while cooking sausage.

I had been in that very basement plenty of times, so I could easily imagine the scene: the complete kitchen and dining area that most Italians had in their homes at that time. But the only thing wrong with that cozy picture was the Cigar dead on the floor. I just couldn't imagine it.

Then I started to recall all the times I'd been with Sam Giancana, starting with those times he would drive me and my brother to school. And then there we were at my father's grave with him asking me to be the First Ward Alderman of Chicago.

So many memories.

And then I recalled the last time I had seen Sam Giancana alive.

It was in the men's room in the basement of the Mercury Theater on North Avenue in Elmwood Park. That's when he told me that he had just been subpoenaed to testify before the Grand Jury. He was worried that they would grant him immunity. He could either go along with them and talk, or refuse to talk and get incarcerated for the term of that particular Grand Jury.

He knew his life wasn't going to be the same again regardless of which course he took. Nobody likes a rat, but then who wants to spend a year in Cook County Jail? What a choice.

Sam also recognized that other people in the Outfit were not happy with all the adverse publicity he had gotten from his association with the likes of Phyllis McGuire, Frank Sinatra, and Marilyn Monroe. He was bringing way too much attention on the organization, and they didn't like it. So Sam knew that he would have to do his time in jail for refusing to testify, and he said that when he was released he might just go away.

And, as you know, he went to Mexico after getting out of Cook County Jail, and he lived there for nine years until the United States government brought him back.

And he was only home about a month when he got the double-whammy of open-heart surgery and a subpoena to appear before the United States Senate Racketeering Committee. And he was just days from appearing before that committee when he got his own Taylor Street Justice in his basement.

Unfortunately, I never got to see Sam Giancana during those last weeks of his life. But when I did see him at the Mercury Theater before he went to Mexico, I sensed it would be our final farewell. He did too.

And so Sam Giancana gave me two pieces of advice during our final meeting that have served me well to this day. "One, all politicians are full of bullshit, and two, don't run again." I failed to heed that second bit of wisdom and did run again, and was re-elected. I should have listened to the Cigar that final time we met. He was right. And he was absolutely right when he said the curtain was closing on organized crime with the advent of the Immunity Law and the Witness Protection Program.

"It would be almost impossible for it to continue much longer," he said.

And he was right, because the Mob began to disintegrate within six years of his death. What's left of it today is a joke.

Oh, I know, the media and movie producers and book publishers would have you believe it is still as powerful as it ever was, but let me tell you the simple truth: the Mob has as much relevance today as Jesse James robbing a stagecoach.

The Mob, like Jesse James, is history.

With Sam Giancana's death came many unanswered questions, foremost being, Who would avenge him and get what Italians call "vendetta?" What would become of those loyal to the Cigar? I can tell you what happened to two of

Giancana's loyalists - they got Taylor Street Justice just like their boss did.

One of Sam's cohorts, Chuckie English, was assassinated in the parking lot of Horwath's Restaurant on North Harlem Avenue in Elmwood Park a few years after Giancana got murdered in his basement.

I knew Chuckie English for many years, and I can say he was one of the best-groomed men I have ever known. My mother always thought he was handsome.

Shortly after Chuckie English got served with some Taylor Street Justice, a second cohort named Chuckie Nicoletti met a similar end in the Golden Horn Restaurant parking lot on North Avenue in Melrose Park.

I knew this Chuckie from when I was a little kid, and I can tell you he was from Lexington, California and had owned a saloon in Chicago called the Little Wheel. It was near Altgeld Park where we played softball, and we often stopped for a cold beer after the game. None of us were 21 or older at the time, but Chuckie would tell the bartender: "Keep these kids full, and don't take any money from them." He was a good guy, and he met his untimely end because he was loyal to Mo Giancana.

I still have plenty of my own questions arising from Sam Giancana's assassination.

For example, could there ever be another organized crime syndicate to rival the Chicago Outfit in terms of power and connections?

I doubt it very much.

Could there ever be another Cigar?

Again, I doubt it very much.

Sure, the Cigar did a lot of good in his lifetime, charity work that nobody ever heard about. But he also did a lot of bad things that everybody heard about.

The man who was born Salvatore Giancana on May 24, 1908, rose to become one of the most powerful men in America.

Who else but Sam Giancana could pick up a phone and have somebody killed in any part of the United States.

Who else but Sam "the Cigar" Giancana would pick up a phone and call a strike against an entire industry?

Who else but Mo could bring the entire film industry to a standstill with one simple phone call?

Here was a man who was born to poor Sicilian immigrants in the "Little Italy" section of Chicago, and rose from that absolute poverty to become the most powerful organized-crime figure in American history.

Al Capone only dreamed of having the power that Sam Giancana wielded every day when he was boss of the Chicago Outfit.

No, there will never be another Sam Giancana.

But gangsters are good for the box office, and their larger-than-life legends make for blockbuster movies and best selling books.

And, to prove my point, they were releasing a

big budget movie about bank robber John Dillinger as I was finishing this book. They even picked an actor, Johnny Depp, who looked just like Dillinger to play the part.

Styling himself as a latter-day Robin Hood, Dillinger was a dangerous criminal who met his end on July 22, 1934 after watching Manhattan Melodrama at the Biograph Theater on Lincoln Avenue in Chicago.

Before he came to Chicago to hide out, Dillinger had to get permission from the crime syndicate, because they didn't want anybody "hot" to be in Chicago. So they told him it would be all right to hide in Chicago so long as he not hit any Chicago banks. Organized crime didn't need that kind of heat.

Dillinger was just one of the many notorious criminals who made big names for themselves during the Great Depression. Names we still remember today like: Two-Gun Kelly, Bonnie and Clyde, and Ma Barker. They might have gotten enough ink to fill ten swimming pools, but they never came close to the Chicago Outfit in terms of power and money.

The Chicago Outfit reached its peak under the leadership of Sam Giancana, and it began its rapid descent to obscurity at his assassination.

The government picked them off, one by one: guilty as charged, guilty as charged, guilty as charged, and so on and so forth.

Two other crime syndicate figures, Jack Cerone and Joey Aiuppa, went to jail for 29 years for skimming money from Las Vegas.

Then the two Spilatro brothers were murdered. The feds, with help from the Outfit itself, simply unraveled the fabric of what had once been a tight-knit organization.

And just recently six or seven men from the old Chinatown crew went to jail, meaning there are no longer any districts. There is no more hierarchy. And there is no more money coming in to anybody from organized crime.

Sure, there will always be criminals. It's human nature.

And the news media will always throw the words "Organized Crime" into headline stories.

If it bleeds, it leads, and nothing sells news better than Organized Crime.

The Mob.

The Syndicate.

The Outfit.

There is big money in those words, and the media knows it. So of course they're not going to erase them from their vocabulary even if those organizations no longer exist.

The Outfit might be gone, but some of the old-timers are still around Chicago, living quietly as law-abiding citizens. They have all the money they need, and they have no more need for Taylor Street Justice.

The curtain came down on their act in the mid 1980s. Again, the feds had the weapons they needed in the Immunity Law and the Witness Protection Program.

Naturally the old-timers will tell you what a time they had in "their day." Their days were filled with excitement and adventure and more money than they could count. I know they have fond memories, but I also know they are happy for their current lives of quiet contentment.

Just as I know that kids from the old neighborhood who chose a life of organized crime did so not because of the money but as a result of social pressure. They wanted to show the tough guys on Taylor Street that they were tough too. And, of course, once they got into the rackets, they learned to like all that money that kept rolling in. Who wouldn't?

And Sam Giancana wasn't the only one who loved the limelight and the power that went with being a made member of the Chicago Outfit. Politicians and reporters listened to you, and beautiful women were at your beck and call.

Who wouldn't love a life like that?

But then quite a few of the people I knew in organized crime were invisible to the public. They were the more intelligent, powerful people. You never heard about them and you never heard from them.

The ones you did read about in the papers and see on television were the underlings who loved the publicity. They just didn't understand that it was not a safe thing to have your mug in the paper all the time or on television. But some of them just loved that limelight, and Sam Giancana was the prime example.

It was so intoxicating he never realized it would be his downfall. Sam Giancana was in the public eye the whole time he was romancing Phyllis McGuire. His associates hated it, because it cast the limelight on them too. They wanted Sam to be discrete, but he would not and could not because he had an enormous ego, as I have already told you.

Why else would he brag to me about electing the President of the United States? It was his ego showing.

Sam would walk into a restaurant, and, instead of sitting quietly in the corner, he would take a table in the middle to let everybody know that "the Cigar" had arrived. Sam did everything to excess, good and bad.

When my mother died, the florist delivered a cross of white orchids that stood 8 feet high and was 6 feet wide. The card only said that it was "from a friend," so I asked the florist, "Who are they from?"

He said, "Well, you know - your friend."

He didn't have to say another word. I knew it was from the Cigar.

Just as I knew that the Cigar had been absolutely right when he advised me not to run for re-election as Alderman of the First Ward. I should have listened to him, because after I got re-elected I saw the power start to wane.

They replaced good-old patronage with a merit

system and Civil Service jobs and tests. Hiring and firing were no longer simple matters, unless you wanted a lawsuit pending against you.

Aldermen no longer could put their own police captains at the head of their districts. The city gave the police a raise to break their dependence on kickbacks from organized crime. Patronage was past history, and aldermen could no longer hire people based on how many votes they could deliver on election day and how much money they could bring to the organization.

So the Alderman of the First Ward was no longer the feared, political powerhouse he had been just seven or eight years prior to the reforms.

But I wonder: did the poor benefit from the breaking up of the "Machine" that the media called corrupt? Was the Machine such a bad thing, after all? Tell me, where does a poor person go today to get a favor? What poor person can go and hire a lawyer to obtain justice?

I always think that they should replace the "s" in justice with a "$," because when you don't have the money you don't get the justice.

Or, as a black counterpart on the City Council used to tell me, "Without no finance, there ain't no romance."

I believe that as long as there are people there will be crime. But I wonder if the public is better off without organized crime, what with our crazy world of the disorganized crimes of wild rapes, house break-ins, muggings, child abuse, and car-jackings.

Today, any crazy can come out of nowhere and put a gun to your head and just blow you away for no good reason. But in their day, organized crime never put a gun to anybody's head and forced them to make a bet or drink bootleg whiskey. They did, of course, expect you to pay if you lost your bet, but what business doesn't collect on its debts?

A priest at St. Malachi's Catholic Church on the West Side of Chicago found through a survey that the public actually got a better payoff from the Outfit's games of chance than from the State of Illinois' legal games of chance known as the lottery.

Go figure.

And you were safer living in a neighborhood with organized crime figures, because they had families too. Like we used to say: "You may rape a girl once in this neighborhood, but you would never rape anybody a second time."

I miss that era of "Taylor Street Justice," and I am more than happy that I was part of it. It was an exciting, interesting adventure.

I am happy I did it, and I am glad I was involved in it all when I was young enough to enjoy it. But I am just as glad that I left that life when I was no longer young enough to enjoy it.

I will remember those amazing times to my dying day, and I will end this chapter on this note: There will never be another Chicago Outfit or another era as exciting as that one.

Good-bye to those days, my friend.

CHAPTER SIXTEEN

POLITICS
(FUTURE SHOCK/FUTURE SCHLOCK)

"It doesn't matter who votes.
It only matters who counts the votes."

"Politics: The last resort of the incompetent."

"When a minority becomes a majority and seizes
authority, they suppress the minority."

"When the fix is in on both sides, justice will prevail."

"You don't go to court to get justice;
you go to court for the chance that you will get justice."

William Parrillo, my father, made that last quote, and was he ever right. Politics, as practiced in this country is strange business, and the 2008 Presidential campaign is a perfect example.

All the Democrats were emphasizing how bad the economy was, but candidate Joe Biden, who is now our Vice President, went on national television and said: "George Bush should have gotten on television like Franklin D. Roosevelt did in 1929 when the Great Crash and Depression started. He quieted down the entire country." That's exactly what the man who is now our Vice President said when he was a candidate in 2008.

How do you excuse such a statement when you consider that Joe Biden has been in public life for more than 30 years, and would certainly seem to know the history of the United States? He certainly understood the Constitution of the United States well enough to know that Article I, Section 3 clearly states that "no person shall be a Senator who shall not have attained to the age of thirty years."

So Joe Biden got himself elected as a Senator from Delaware at 29 and conveniently turned 30 before the Senate's next session. With all that knowledge of the Constitution and American History, you would think that the learned Senator from Delaware would have known that people didn't have televisions in 1929, and that Franklin Roosevelt wasn't elected President until November 1932.

Roosevelt, of course, first took office in 1933,

but Joe Biden didn't seem to know that. He was off by, oh, say, three years. A minor mistake except when you're running for the second highest office in the land.

I shudder to think that an incompetent like this is only a heartbeat away from the Presidency. Long live President Barack Obama!

If Presidential elections can be fixed, then why not local zoning matters. Like they say, "When the fix is in on both sides justice will prevail."

Let me tell you about a classic fixed case right here in Chicago:

Once upon a time, the building inspector for the City of Chicago in charge of factories and commercial structures ticketed a south side factory for code violations amounting to about $160,000. The owner was a friend, so he asked me for help.

Here is how the case was resolved: The judge assigned to the case had a son who was in his first year of college in downstate Illinois. Annual tuition at that time was about $8,000, and the judge's son had three more years to go. So my friend's company agreed to donate $24,000 to the college so the judge's son would have a three-year scholarship and thus earn his degree. I prevailed upon the city factory inspector and the Corporation Counsel's Office not to "pursue" the case, and, miracle of miracles, the complaint was dismissed.

The judge was happy because he did not have to accept a dime. The judge's son was happy because he got to complete his college education. The company was happy because they deducted the $24,000 from their income tax as a "donation." And the Alderman was really happy when his friend's company put a non-interest bearing deposit of $100,000 in his bank.

My list of such stories about politics is endless. But I have my own thoughts to share with you now as we close out my first book.

I ran for elected office, was elected to that office, and proudly served as First Ward Alderman in Chicago. So I have often been asked by many a Political Science professor to speak to his or her class. I was flattered to get such invitations, but I told them all that by the time I gave the lecture and told the truth about politics, they wouldn't have any students left in their classes.

But a professor at the University of Illinois Chicago wouldn't take no for an answer and said he himself wanted to hear what I would say to his students about my views on politics. So I went to what we used to call "Circle Campus" and began my lecture by holding up a dollar bill in my hand and telling the class, "This is the bottom line of politics."

The faces on those young, idealistic students dropped immediately. After all, they still thought George Washington had not chopped down that cherry tree.

So I did a spot survey of who was liberal, conservative, and middle-of-the road in the class. Most of the kids raised their hands when I asked who the liberals were.

Young people are like that; they think the

government is a panacea for all our problems.

Needless to say, the conservatives and middle-of-the-roaders were seriously outnumbered. Then I asked for a volunteer to stand up and submit to my questions. A very bright young lady popped right up, and so I asked her: "Do you believe in one person, one vote?"

"Oh, definitely," she said. "That's the basis of our democracy."

"All right," I said, "then explain this to me. The State of California has a population of 35 million and two United States Senators. That means that 17,500,000 people in California get one vote in the United States Senate. Wyoming has about 500,000 people, and, like California, they have two United States Senators. So people in Wyoming get one vote in the United Senate per every 250,000 people. Now, you tell me where there is one person, one vote in our democracy."

That bright young student couldn't tell me.

So I asked her, "Why do we need a United States Senate?"

She didn't really know, nor did the other students in the class. So I explained the real world of politics to them, beginning with the Founding Fathers who provided for a Senate in the Constitution because they assumed it would be easier to defeat a Senator in a statewide election than a member of the House of Representative in his local district.

Why? Because of the money it would take to campaign statewide and because they knew a local

Congressman would be popular with the hometown folks in his district. The House of Representatives is, after all, proportionately representative of the people. The House made sense, but why we ended up with the United States Senate I do not understand to this day. It is simply not representative of democracy.

By the way, did you know that Senators were not originally elected by the people of their states? No, they were appointed to their lofty posts by the good old boys back in their state legislatures. Can you imagine the deal making that went on in those musty old chambers?

After that sobering news about the Senate, I simply had to tell those idealistic young students that democracies typically last for about 200 years before committing suicide. I wondered then and I wonder now if that isn't the path we're on now.

When Republican Barry Goldwater challenged the incumbent, Lyndon B. Johnson, for President of the United States, the Democrats accused him of being an "ultra conservative." And, according to the standards of the day, he probably was.

But Goldwater defended himself saying he was running on the same platform that Franklin D. Roosevelt ran on in 1932. Meaning that the conservative of today would have been a liberal 25 years ago, and would have been a "super liberal" 50 years ago. And especially in light of the 2008 election, it seems our nation is trending toward liberalism and the more liberal Democratic Party.

But the Republicans are moving to the left too.

The death knell of a democracy is sounded when its citizens realize they can vote themselves all the goodies they want. What do you think we're doing in this land of excess today?

I got quite the political education when I served on the Chicago City Council as First Ward Alderman, and I particularly remember the time 20th Ward Alderman Ken Campbell asked a group of us: "What's the first criteria of a great statesman?"

We all had different opinions and said you had to be a churchman, or a quarterback for Notre Dame, or just plain Irish.

Alderman Campbell, who was black, shook his head at our answers and said, "The first criteria of a great statesman is the ability to be elected."

I wish he had been with me at the Political Science Class at University of Illinois Chicago. Alderman Campbell would have really poked some big holes in their idealism. I did honor him by posing that same question to the students, and they said you had to be a great speechmaker to get elected, or good-looking like John F. Kennedy. You had to do this, and you had to do that.

They all had answers and opinions, so I set them straight by saying, "Some people are a product of a political machine; some are the products of the very wealthy people in the area who want them elected only to serve their selfish interests, not the common good."

Being a product of the former, I gave them a tutorial on the famous First Ward of yesteryear where we had approximately 30,000 votes and

between 7,000 and 8,000 people on the city, county and state payrolls. For about half of those jobs,
you didn't even have to show up for work. "And we
used to measure every job as three votes per job,"
I told the students. "The other part of it would be
that businessmen would pay their workers on our
behalf, or bookmakers would spread money
throughout the ward on election day. It mattered
little or nothing to the people who was running or
what their platform was. Hardly anybody ever
cared anyway. All they knew is that because of the
Alderman, they were able to bring home a pay-
check." Those young jaws dropped even lower.

And so I continued to amaze them by telling
them that the First Ward could deliver 25,000
votes to Attila the Hun if he was on the ballot. I
don't think he ever was, but you might want to
check. Their eyes widened as I went on about the
real nature of "Machine Politics" in Chicago. All
the great things they had read about George Washington and Abraham Lincoln were twirling in their
heads. Could their heroes have been the same way?
Could the men on the one and five dollar bills have
been in it for the money?

"Nothing changes," I told them. "Money will
always be the bottom line of politics. The difference will be the way people are elected."

I explained to the students that the "Machine"
and its patronage system was coming to an end. I
told them that federal laws like the Immunity Act
and the one that created the Witness Protection
Program were crushing a crime syndicate that had

once controlled the infamous "River Wards" where votes were weighed, not counted. I was right on both counts.

The students wanted to know what would replace the old way.

Fair question, but first I had to explain how it had been "in our day" when, if you wanted to be a candidate in the First Ward, you went hat-in-hand to the State Street Council.

At that time, they represented about 12 major department stores. Those stores in turn were the leading advertisers in Chicago's six daily newspapers. So they could "pressure" any of those newspapers by collectively withdrawing their ads.

So naturally when the State Street Council wanted a particular candidate to be elected, every newspaper in Chicago would tell you what a wonderful human being he was, even though he didn't know what he was doing, much less care about the people he was going to represent.

I was an exception because I did care about the people in my ward. But State Street, of course, didn't care about the people. The merchant class never mingled with poor people or got calls in the middle of the night like I did as Alderman. They didn't have to go down to the police station and bail out a voter's son or daughter. They didn't have to do favors for the little people because they were the big people.

There's really only one department store left on State Street now, and there are shopping malls all over the suburbs, so the State Street Council is a shadow of its former self. So, I asked the students, how does one get elected today?

They didn't know, so I presented a hypothetical situation in which John Jones is seeking an important office but lacks the big bucks needed to get elected. "The conclusion," I said, "is that John Jones can't run for an important office. He's shut out."

John Jones and those like him can no longer turn to a powerful political machine, organized crime, or labor unions for support. They all exist in the imagination of the news media, but they no longer have the political muscle to put their chosen people in office. Our current President proved the power of the Internet and blogs when he got elected in 2008.

Newspapers were not big players in that election, and even television has lost its clout. You talk to young people today, and they'll tell you that they get ALL their news on-line. One young lady even said, "You're really in if you never watch news on television."

So how do you get elected in this brave new world of the Internet and Twitter and who knows what? People are completely bypassing newspapers and television stations and exchanging ideas and information on the Internet. And just imagine the amazing ways with which our children and grandchildren will exchange news and information.

Barack Obama proved himself to be a master of this new technology, and that's why he's sitting in the White House today as the 44th President of the United States.

Good for him, but, in my humble opinion, now that the election is over nothing has changed.

And nothing will change.

In my opinion, there are only two, three-letter words that rule the country and the world: "s-e-x" and "o-i-l."

Sex and oil. The big multi-national corporations control the oil, and they control all the candidates, and they decide who gets elected.

This reminds me of the prize-fight promoter who owns both boxers. He hypes up the boxing match to sell his tickets. Then, when the fight starts, he's sitting in his ticket office counting the receipts, not caring who wins the fight. He wins no matter who wins. And so it is with the big corporations who own both candidates. Especially in Presidential elections. They have the media to remake you overnight into whatever they think will sell: conservative or a liberal. They can even change your height and weight. These corporations are powerful, powerful entities. And when you add it all up, the people have little or nothing to say about any candidate.`

So imagine those dewy-eyed students sitting there at Circle listening to me tell them like it was, is, and will forever be. I was not your typical speaker from the chamber of commerce, and I told them this simple truth: THE LAST TIME I VOTED WAS FOR MYSELF. That's right, and I will probably never vote again.

Why? Let me tell you: When Goldwater and Johnson were vying for the presidency in 1964,

I was going up the elevator to my office at 330 South Wells Street. The elevator operator was an old-timer named Chester who asked me what I thought about the election. "Johnson will beat Goldwater badly."

I was right, of course, but I always liked to get the opinions of the common man, so I asked Chester whom he was voting for and why.

"Lyndon Johnson," he said, "because he does what he says he's gonna do, and that to me is a great politician."

And, just as I predicted, Johnson went on to trounce Goldwater in the November election.

And so I found myself riding the elevator with Chester after the election, and he said, "That damn Lyndon Johnson."

"What are you angry about? You voted for him. You wanted him to win."

"Yeah, but now he's giving everything to the blacks."

Johnson was promoting civil rights legislation at that time, so Chester had a point. So I said, "Well, Chester, when he was running for office, he said that he was going to promote civil rights and help the African-American people of this country. This should come as no surprise."

Chester confounded me with his answer, saying, "Yeah, but I didn't think he'd do it."

That reminds me of an expression we had in the First Ward that most of the Polish people are Republicans 364 days a year, but become Democrats on election day. They were back to being

Republicans the next day and complaining about the Democrats. Go figure.

Like I told those students at Circle, modern politics makes no sense to me. How, for example, do we allow people who can't even balance their checkbooks to tell us which presidential candidate will fix the economy? Why do we let leaders with no military experience send our troops to foreign countries to fight "our" wars? Who decides where they go and what they're fighting for? And what about appointing justices to the United States Supreme Court? They appoint certain people with certain philosophies of the Constitution, and the average person has no knowledge of the law or its application.

I could cite thousands of examples of why campaigns are not logical, and why people have no idea who they are voting for or why. But it really doesn't matter. Nothing is going to change.

Corporate America will continue to control the country, and they are not about to ask you and me for our opinions. But we will continue to work for them and do as we're told.

As I told those bright-eyed college students at the University of Illinois Chicago, election day is the day that the rich people in America let the poor people entertain themselves by thinking they've got something to say about whom will run America and how it will be run.

All that's missing on election day is some myth-ical figure like Santa Claus or the Easter Bunny reminding the poor saps to go out and vote.

That's the way it is, and that's the way it will be. Nothing will change.

And it will be no different from the old days when you had the State Street Council wielding all that power over the newspapers with their mighty advertising dollars. They never said publicly that they favored the First Ward, but they never privately opposed a First Ward Alderman. They would just let the election go, knowing that the First Ward was going to dominate the other wards.

In return for their support, we would ensure that there was more than enough police protection for parades because we didn't want to ruin the image of State Street. Then, as soon as the parade was finished, we would have street cleaners shovel up the horse manure, sweep up the debris, and take down the barriers. In the winter, we saw that their sidewalks were shoveled, and we even cleaned their underground driveways.

Sure, we even paved their private driveways, which, of course, we were not supposed to do. But who was going to tell the public?

When the CHICAGO DAILY NEWS building on Madison Street by the river flooded, who manned the pumps but the Chicago Fire Department. Not their job, but the media went right along because they were part of the system too.

When I was Alderman, I gave the Palmer House Hotel something no one else on State Street had at the time, a liquor license to a restaurant that opened to State Street. No one objected, and it was for a high-class restaurant, so naturally we were in favor of it also. We saved the Palmer House serious money by plowing and cleaning their sidewalks.

The Palmer House in turn spoke kindly of us in the press, and they even remained silent on the subject of a certain bookmaking joint at the corner of State and Van Buren. It was right down the street from the Palmer House, and they could have made a big stink about it in the press, but they didn't.

As I have said repeatedly in this book and will probably say repeatedly in future books, the so-called gangsters of the crime syndicate are no different from the Senators and Congressman who sit across from them during their investigations.

Again, I would always rate a crime syndicate figure higher on the morality scale than a politician. That's my opinion, and I'm sticking with it.

So, what is the future of politics in the United States of America?

That was the $10 million question in that classroom at Chicago Circle that day, and it remains a pressing issue.

To look forward, I have to look back to when I was Alderman of the First Ward when backers would make donations of $500 or even $1,000 out of friendship. But when the big real estate developers said they wanted to donate $100,000 I knew they sure as hell didn't believe in good government. They wanted a zoning change or a permit or a quick end to whatever "little problem" they might be having.

Money was the most important thing in politics then, and it is still true today.

My crystal ball says that the successful politician of tomorrow will be the one who raises enough money to create the image he needs to get elected. And that image can vary from liberal to conservative to middle-of-the-road depending on what Corporate America wants the poor people to "think" on election day.

Remember though, for every dollar our successful politician of tomorrow will collect, he will incur an obligation to powerful people with very deep pockets. They will expect payback from their political star once he or she has attained office, and they will surely get it.

If I sound cynical, it is because I have dissected too many modern campaign promises. Say a candidate says, "I'm for lower taxes."

Well, you go and look at his record and see that he has consistently voted for higher taxes.

Gee, how did that not get reported?

Well, do you own a major media outlet?

No, of course not. The media are owned by Corporate America, and they dish out the news that their corporate masters tell them to dish out. They represent themselves, but they do want you as part of their audience, so they make their programs as tantalizing as they can. The bigger the audience, the bigger the ad rates. Simple arithmetic, really.

So the only real watchdogs of the people are the people themselves. But only half of us even bother to vote. As one who hasn't voted in decades, I understand the frustration and disillusionment that leads to not voting. You vote for a candidate because he reportedly backs your position on an issue, and you like him because he's a member of your ethnic group, but then, come election day, he's changed his tune completely. No wonder less than 50 percent of the people vote.

Bill O'Reilly, who is the most popular newscaster on cable television, said shortly after we went to war in Iraq that, "of course, no president wants a war." How naive. The truth of the matter is that every president wants an excuse to go to war.

War creates jobs, helps our economy, and it helps the president get re-elected. War gives him a chance to be a hero. I would hope that people would have sense enough to see so-called "news" for what it really is: entertainment.

It doesn't matter what format - print or electronic - it is entertainment, pure and simple. But I doubt people will see it as such, because everyone likes to be entertained.

And both liberal and conservative news programs present their own agendas. Neither side is objective and unbiased.

And, in my humble opinion, there are far more liberal newscasters than conservative ones.

And, as I reminded those students at Circle, nothing will change.

I told them how Franklin Roosevelt had promised in his 1940 campaign for re-election as President that he would "not send our boys overseas." But he did!

Lyndon Johnson and Hubert Humphrey made Barry Goldwater out to be a "warmonger" in the 1964 election, but then, after they won, they turned around and sent all the American boys they could to Vietnam. Even as they were running as men of peace, Johnson and Humphrey were planning to expand the undeclared war in Vietnam.

George Herbert Walker Bush promised the American public, "Read my lips, no new taxes." Then, as soon as he was elected the 41st President of the United States, he raised our taxes.

Here's another example of what I'm talking about: When a precinct captain in the First Ward would pay some very poor person living in the projects a few dollars for his vote, the media would magnify this terrible crime and demand that everyone involved be indicted.

But when one candidate for the President of the United States makes an agreement with a rival candidate that she withdraw from the campaign in return for being appointed Secretary of State and having her $20 million campaign debt paid off, that's just fine.

As for me, I fail to see any difference between those two transactions, only the price.

Ah, Democracy, I love it!

I say all this as the "man for all seasons" who grew up in a poor but ethnically cohesive neighborhood and worked my way to a share of the American dream. I knew seasons of poverty, and I knew and know seasons of wealth. I am as American as they come. But people kidded me because in the course of one day I could rub shoulders with the Mayor of Chicago and the Governor of Illinois at a downtown dedication and then retreat to the old Taylor Street neighborhood for an afternoon crap game in the alley.

Well, this is the end of my little adventure in print. I hope it was as interesting and informative as it was for me, "the man for all seasons."

And remember, the last time I ever voted was for Alderman Donald W. Parrillo, First Ward, City of Chicago.

Those students that day at University of Illinois Chicago asked me if I would ever run for Mayor of Chicago. Reporters and newscasters often asked me the same question.

I had one answer for all of them and for you too: "Who in the hell would want to be Mayor of the City of Chicago when you can be Alderman of the First Ward?"

Goodbye until we meet again in my next book. I have just begun to write!

CAPONE MAY GO FREE
www.caponemaygofree.com
1.877.874.6220

CAPONE MAY GO FREE PUBLISHING
208 Pine Lake Avenue
Suite 211
LaPorte, Indiana
46350
publishing@caponemaygofree.com